VGM Opportunities Series

OPPORTUNITIES IN
ARCHITECTURAL
CAREERS

Robert J. Piper
Richard D. Rush

Foreword by
W. Cecil Steward FAIA
President
The American Institute of Architects

 **VGM Career Horizons**
a division of *NTC Publishing Group*
Lincolnwood, Illinois USA

Cover Photo Credits

Front cover: upper left, Susan Maxman, FAIA;
upper right, lower left, and lower right, The
Chicago Architecture Foundation.

Back cover: upper left, Van Inwegen photo,
courtesy of Chicago Architecture Foundation;
upper right, NTC print; lower left, Chicago
Architecture Foundation.

Library of Congress Cataloging-in-Publication Data

Piper, Robert J.
    Opportunities in architecture careers / Robert J. Piper, Richard
D. Rush.

        p.   cm. — (VGM opportunities series)
    Includes bibliographical references.
    ISBN 0-8442-4038-9 — ISBN 0-8442-4039-7 (pbk.)
    1. Architecture—Vocational guidance—United States. I. Rush,
Richard D. (Richard David), 1944–   . II. Title. III. Series.
NA1995.P5   1992
720'.23'73—dc20   92-20018
                                                          CIP

Published by VGM Career Horizons, a division of NTC Publishing Group.
© 1993 by NTC Publishing Group, 4255 West Touhy Avenue,
Lincolnwood (Chicago), Illinois 60646-1975 U.S.A.
All rights reserved. No part of this book may be reproduced, stored
in a retrieval system, or transmitted in any form or by any means,
electronic, mechanical, photocopying, recording or otherwise, without
the prior permission of NTC Publishing Group.
Manufactured in the United States of America.

2 3 4 5 6 7 8 9 0 VP 9 8 7 6 5 4 3 2 1

ABOUT THE AUTHOR

Richard D. Rush, AIA, is an architect, editor, and educator residing in Glendale, California.

As an editor, he has experience in magazines and books. For three years he was Director of Technical Information for the American Institute of Architects and editor of the award-winning book *The Building Systems Integration Handbook,* available internationally. Prior to employment on the AIA national staff, he was a Senior Editor for four years with *Progressive Architecture* magazine. As a freelance writer, his work has appeared in prominent architectural publications in the U.S. as well as Australia and Italy. As founding acquisitions editor at Butterworth Architecture, a British-based international publisher, he secured contracts for 22 new books and the *Journal of Architectural Education.*

He has lectured at over thirty schools of architecture, as well as numerous industry conferences and architectural firms. His teaching includes a variety of workshops and courses. Recent invitations include lectures at the Moscow Institute of Architecture and the Paris office of Ricardo Bofill. His faculty appointments include positions at Carnegie-Mellon University and the Massachusetts Institute of Technology. He is currently Coordinator of the Technology Curriculum and Associate Professor of Architecture at Woodbury University.

Mr. Rush is a registered architect in the United States with NCARB Certification. His recent architectural firm employment includes The Architects Collaborative (TAC) in Cambridge, Massachusetts, and the office of Earl R. Flansburgh & Associates in Boston. His current consulting work centers around building systems integration.

Mr. Rush received his Bachelor of Architecture degree from the Massachusetts Institute of Technology and his Master of Architecture degree from the Cranbrook Academy of Art. He also served as a rural housing volunteer in the United States Peace Corps in the Ivory Coast.

FOREWORD

So you're thinking about becoming an architect? Well, hurry up; the 21st century needs you.

There are schools, hospitals, and places of worship to be built. There is affordable quality housing to be designed that dignifies the people who live inside. There are communities and whole cities to be turned around by design to bring us together as a people instead of separating us by fear.

There are mass transportation systems that need the logic that only design can bring. There are the handicapped—whether by accident, illness, or age—who need access to the life around them so they can make their contributions to a society that can no longer afford their dependent isolation. And there's our historic fabric of older buildings, which needs our creative stewardship if we are not to lose the history, the values, and, yes, the beauty that give us roots and a sense of belonging.

More than ever we need the special gifts architects bring as problem solvers—gifts distinguished by a unique responsiveness to art and science, the heart and the head. We need these gifts not only in the architect's office, but in the schools as teachers who inspire, in banking as informed advisers for critical financial decisions, in corporate America where the products we produce for a global market demand a competitive design edge, and in legislative halls as representatives of the people.

Architecture is a way of thinking about the environment. As such, architects are in the most profound sense environmentalists. Their work has a direct bearing on how all of us use fixed and renewable resources, how we use energy, and how we leave our thumbprint on the land. When a neighborhood or a community struggles to define a vision of what it wants to be, it's the architect who can transform abstract words into an image of a better, shared future.

If this is how you see yourself, read on.

The author of this book will tell you becoming an architect isn't easy. It isn't. There are long hours in the classroom and years of internship. Even then the learning never stops because the technology of architecture is changing ever more rapidly at the same time that the art of architecture challenges and redefines the boundaries of the human imagination.

There are disappointments, frustrations, and endless compromises. The regulatory climate in which architecture grows blows hot, then cold. Economic cycles are even more harsh.

Yet these very challenges together with the commitment to lifelong learning about yourself and the world around you as well as the responsibility of serving human needs keep the mind agile and the spirit young. Look at the work of those architects you most admire; almost without exception their ideas become more daring, more imaginative, more charged with an astonishing vigor the older they get.

If you're up to the long hours of hard work, if you're committed to serving others, if you're enthusiastic about the world around you and have a thirst for ideas, if you see yourself as someone who could make a better life for people, you have the most important prerequisites to embark on the adventure of your life.

Read on.

> W. Cecil Steward FAIA
> President
> The American Institute of Architects

CONTENTS

Creating the human environment. You and architecture. Architecture—past and present. Architecture—future challenge. The construction industry. Constructing a high school. The environmental design professions. Career options. Need for personnel. Automation. Age limitations. Opportunities for women. Earnings. Educational requirements. Licensing. Career choice and career opportunity.

The public interest. Requirements of the profession. The profession of architecture. The vocation of architecture. Attitudes, motivations, and aptitudes. To be an architect.

CHAPTER 1

OUR PHYSICAL ENVIRONMENT

CREATING THE HUMAN ENVIRONMENT

In the most simple terms, architecture is the art and science of designing buildings and the spaces between them. However, this definition is much too simple because the spaces referred to dictate how we move about and carry out our everyday activities, and, therefore, these spaces are an extremely important part of our physical environment. Architecture *is* environment; it is with us all the time—we live in it, play in it, work in it, and are seldom free from its influence. It is, perhaps, one of the two or three most important influences on our lives.

Given this importance, it is important that a sense of quality should permeate the work of an architect. Certainly, we are all interested in quality in all that we do. However, those who would practice architecture have a particular responsibility for producing quality work. After all, if architecture is one of the principal influences shaping human and community progress, a concern for quality must be uppermost in the minds of those who would practice architecture.

While those who choose architecture are choosing a career in creating the human environment, architects do not perform all of the work required to create that environment; engineers, urban planners, landscape architects, construction contractors, brick masons, carpenters, financiers, building product manufacturers, and many others share in this endeavor. However, architecture is the basic art, the basic science, underlying the creation of the constructed environment. Thus, those trained in architecture will have available to them many and varied career opportunities. This first chapter examines those opportunities.

YOU AND ARCHITECTURE

Look around you. Have you ever noticed the room in which you are now sitting: its size and shape, the height of its ceiling, the distance between its walls and the placement of its doors and windows, texture and patterns of its wall and floor materials, and how it fits in with other rooms in the building? Chances are the room is unique; you probably can't think of another one just like it. It's like your friends—no two are alike. This uniqueness makes this room and the building of which it is a part a special place to you.

Now, if you look out the window and imagine yourself walking down the street passing your window, you realize the street and the buildings facing on it are different from all the others in your town. Yet, all together, these physical elements provide you with a room you know is yours, a house you feel is home, a school that is your own, a friendly neighborhood, a city of which you are proud, a country you love. These feelings result largely from your physical environment—the architectural surroundings in which you live, work, and play.

Now consider the details of your environment—the rug at your feet, the backyard bench, the street lamp at the corner. These too, in all their varied sizes, colors, and textures, are part of your environment. They are the furnishings placed about in the architecture for your convenience and pleasure. They are the individual touches that mark these spaces as belonging to you alone or to your neighborhood alone. Architecture without such furnishings would be incomplete.

Then there are the vistas, sounds, smells, and weather that are part of your environment. In the countryside, architecture has nothing to do with creating these, but it can shape your experience of them to your advantage. Some, like a Nebraska sunset, a Gulf sea breeze, or a Michigan pine scent, you should be able to enjoy freely. Architecture should protect you from other natural elements, such as the bite of a Dakota winter or a humid Missouri summer. In the city, architecture has a great deal to do with creating as well as shaping parts of your environment. The glitter and noise of America's Park Avenues contribute to its architecture as do the grime of its industrial areas and the wretchedness of its slums.

Finally, and perhaps most importantly, your friends are also a part of your environment—a very large part indeed. Architecture is nothing without people; when all is said and done, architecture and the physical environment that it creates are for people. This should never be forgotten.

ARCHITECTURE—PAST AND PRESENT

Beyond your present-day environment lie generations of work by architect-builders of yesteryear. The work of providing shelter stretches back to the first people who piled stone upon stone, instinctively erecting a simple shelter for protection from enemies and the elements. That work, crude as it may seem today, was architecture; those early people were architects.

As people developed, their architectural horizons and technical abilities broadened, until today we are able to enclose entire cities in a single structure. With each historical period in this development, we can associate at least one particular form or style of architecture. These styles are always the result of three basic kinds of characteristics:

Natural Characteristics. Climate, attitude, geography, geology, and plant life. These determine what building materials are locally available and the requirements for weather protection in building construction.

Cultural Characteristics. Religious beliefs, patterns of trade, economy, and government, social ideals, and daily living habits. These determine the functions and activities to be accommodated in building design.

Technical Characteristics. Techniques and methods of structural support. There are three basic structural forms: post and beam, truss, and arch. These determine the means by which spaces are spanned, which in turn determine the open or column-free areas that can be contained within a building unit.

Knowing these characteristics, the architectural historian or archaeologist can identify a building with its place in the history of civilization. Thus, the significance of architectural styles is that they are a reflection of the period in which they evolved—of the people who lived then; their beliefs and aspirations, their environment, and their degree of cultural and technical achievement.

Architecture, as we think of it in terms of our western culture, first appeared some six thousand years ago in Mesopotamia, a wedge of land between the Tigris and Euphrates Rivers in the country now called Iraq. The Babylonians and Assyrians who lived there believed in living for the moment and gave little thought to life after death. Consequently, their architecture was one of lush palaces and other structures reflecting the everyday pleasures they valued. Mesopotamia was rich in clay, river water, and sunshine, but provided little stone or timber, so sun-dried clay brick was a principal building material. Brick surfaces are easily molded into decorative forms, or glazed with colored ceramic materials, or veneered with stone for decoration and weather protection. So, major Babylonian buildings were covered with bas-relief carvings, glazed friezes, or tooled stone veneers depicting incidents in the history of their civilization. Lacking quantities of stone or timber, these people could not span wide distances, and their buildings contained many columned spaces and small rooms. Had they known of the arch they could have vaulted large spaces even with brick. But the arch was not generally known or widely used until the early Romans first successfully employed it around 700 B.C.

Around 3000 B.C., the Egyptian civilization began in the Nile Valley. The people of the valley, in contrast to those in Mesopotamia, believed that their everyday activities should be spent largely in preparation for life after death. Their tombs, in the form of pyramids and large rooms carved out of solid rock hillsides, were created to protect the deceased in their journey through eternal life.

Stone, a material of great crushing strength, is abundant in the Nile Valley. The Egyptians used it in quantity to construct post-and-beam buildings of great mass and height. These architectural forms were appropriate to their belief in the majesty and permanence of eternal life. These bold forms combined with the brilliant sunshine to cause violent light and shadow patterns, which accentuated the massive design of the structures. The dry desert climate has preserved many Egyptian architectural masterpieces to this day.

The Greek Empire during its Hellenic period (700–146 B.C.) brought the architectural foundation of our western culture to full flower. The Greek form of government, academic and philosophical concepts, and cultivation of the arts combined to produce one of the world's great civilizations. Their architecture reflected this achievement; their buildings were proportioned and detailed to a perfection of simplicity and harmony. Part of their success can be attributed to the availability of marble, a strong and beautiful building material that lends itself to exact detailing and fine surface treatment. These materials in the hands of artisans who valued the arts, freedom of mind and spirit, and personal achievement provided the ingredients for architectural excellence. The Greeks principally used a post-and-beam structural system, although they did introduce the truss for spanning large central building spaces. The gable roofs of many of their buildings reflected this structural element.

While the Greeks refined their aesthetics and used a "pure" geometry of circles, squares, and proportional systems, the Romans developed shapes based upon the demands of large-scale structures. They invented the advanced geometry of the ellipse, concrete, and the arch to produce monumental plazas bordered by heavily decorated buildings with huge vaulted interiors (500 B.C.–500 A.D.).

During the Middle Ages, superstitions and distrust caused people of that time to withdraw behind the walls of heavily fortified cities or to crowd around the massive masonry walls of monasteries or the castle of a feudal lord (400–1100 A.D.). People depended on the monasteries or castles for protection; these structures were frequently sited on hilltops that provided sweeping views of the surrounding countryside and early warning of any approaching hostile force. Thick, high masonry walls topped with battlements reinforced the feeling of protection. Masons became extremely skillful, extending the use of stone even to roof construction, in which vaults employing the principle of the arch were used to span increasingly larger spaces. This time was known as the Romanesque Period. The spread of Christianity and the rebirth of scholarship is reflected in the period's development of the church plan based upon the Latin Cross, the ornamentation of doors and windows with carvings depicting religious figures, and the production of incredibly beautiful manuscripts describing the history and growth of the Christian movement.

During the early 1200s, the fear and distrust of the Middle Ages began to give way to the need for greater communication and travel necessitated by increased commerce between cities. Feudal lords combined their resources, and the city-state emerged. People became interested in the world around them and set out to explore what made humanity and nature work. This was the Renaissance Age. Its renewed interest in Greek and Roman cultural concepts including classic architecture reflected the classicism and humanism now associated with the period (1200–1500 A.D.).

During this time, builders became less interested in protection as an element of building design and construction and became intrigued with pushing the performance of masonry to its limits. They emphasized height by using pointed arches and tall slender columns that soared from the floor to the peak of the building. They found they could punch great holes in the sidewalls by placing flying buttresses on the outside of the building to support the inner walls. They filled the openings with magnificent stained glass creations depicting events in human development. Thus, this period of gothic architecture was the ideal reflection of the western world's concurrent interest in expanding knowledge of and influence on nature and culture.

The age of exploration and colonization spread Western European cultural characteristics throughout the world, and in our own hemisphere, we can note countless examples where these European influences combined with those of the American frontier to produce architectural styles unique to the New World (1300–1900).

During this same period, the powerful European monarchies competing for control of the New World rose to heights of unparalleled power in their own countries, and the architecture of such palaces as Windsor, Versailles, and El Escorial reflected their kingly stature. Political and social changes removed most of these monarchies during the early years of the Industrial Revolution, shifting their power to varying forms of democratic government and their wealth to private industrial complexes (1700–present). The architecture of modern-day America is a reflection of value our civilization places on private industry and democracy.

Thus, parallels between the characteristics of historical periods and the architecture they produced can be traced in every age of human development, including our own. As a final example, consider your own high school or college building. It is probably a prominent structure in your community. It is built of materials readily available in your time and your area; it accommodates academic, athletic, and cultural activities that your community believes are important to your way of life; it incorporates contemporary structural techniques devised for enclosing the spaces required to house these activities. The architectural style of your school is a reflection of your time, your town, your beliefs, and your capabilities; its architect was a recorder of time, writing in the most appropriate materials available.

ARCHITECTURE—FUTURE CHALLENGE

Your lifetime already includes interplanetary exploration and, perhaps, may include colonization. Here on Earth, undersea communities are foreseen. You can be sure that the styles of architecture developed during your lifetime will reflect these activities, for our nearly unlimited technical capacity to match dreams with reality is restricted only by the growing need for more intelligent conservation of our ever-scarcer environmental resources.

In thinking about the future, we should not undervalue the need for conservation of those resources. Intelligent concern for conservation will require increasing discipline from those who are responsible for advising society on the use of our limited resources. Fortunately, technological advancements—particularly in communications—make a much more refined use of our scarce resources possible. Moreover, improvements in communications and in the manipulation of basic data should provide us with earlier and more extensive information on the availability of scarce resources, therefore providing us with increasingly frequent cautions on the use of those resources.

If we regard this discipline as positive, we can see that our scientific development is taking us toward the time when we will be able to control our natural environment— or at least very large chunks of it. For instance, we now can enclose entire cities within a single structure, and we are preparing to build minienvironments in space and undersea. These developments in the control of our climate and life resources will have vast effects upon our physical environment and the architecture accommodating that environment. The architects of your generation will respond to this challenge. If, in their response, they develop an architecture that is truly appropriate to its time, its place, and its function, they will have created an architectural style as valid and important as was the Greek, Gothic, or any other historical style.

We best remember each past civilization at its moment of greatest achievement; that moment in history when the cultural elements of the civilization—its social, moral, ethical, political, and technical achievements—all seemed to be in balance. We also know that each civilization waned when these elements got out of balance. The architecture of a civilization is a reflection of this balance or imbalance.

The years since the end of World War II have seen immense changes in the way we look at our physical environment and in the manner in which we attempt to manipulate it for our own enjoyment and convenience. In the late 1940s through early 1960s, we sensed there was scarcely any technical challenge that we could not overcome given the seemingly limitless technical expertise and natural resources available to us. Indeed, that remarkable period of innovation and growth produced a number of new building types intimately reflective of our feelings about the security of the present and the promise of the future. The interstate expressway system, the regional shopping center, the totally new suburban community, the international airport, the integrated petrochemical complex, the nuclear power plant, the fantasy-land family recreation complex, the urban renewal project that completely rebuilt large chunks of our older cities, and the mixed-use urban developments are all examples of the remarkable vigor and energy so typical of those years. The architecture of these projects reflected the time. Structural systems, mechanical systems, enclosure systems, graphics and signage systems, materials, and furnishings all became increasingly simplified and stripped down to their essentials in an effort to match productive capacities to the demands of a market that required buildings to accommodate increasingly large, complex functions. Mass production became an end in itself, and much of our physical environment seemed to take on a sameness or commonality: one housing area seemed to look like all the rest, one could perceive little difference between the newer office buildings, each airport terminal was nearly indistinguishable from another. In the late 1960s and early 1970s, architecture's modern movement had reached a point where it seemed that its further refinement would produce little or no true advancement in the art and science of architecture.

A modern movement had become institutionalized as a direct reflection of what had happened to our society in general. In the late 1960s and early 1970s, society reacted, sometimes violently, seeking to change our institutions by giving greater recognition to the value of diversity and worth of the individual. Concurrently, we discovered that our resources were limited and that money and technology alone could not solve all our contemporary problems. The conservation movement, the equal rights movement, the citizen participation movement, and a host of other societal concerns regarding criminal justice, health planning, the elderly, the handicapped, and community and family history all are products of this fervor. These phenomena have had their effect on architecture.

One of the most notable effects has been the growth in the rehabilitation and restoration of existing structures. The tremendous growth in our economy following World War II promoted an almost universal attitude that new was better than old, and a basic assumption that growth could only be accommodated in new, fresh structures placed upon previously undeveloped land. "Technological obsolescence" in building materials and systems were seen as the prime criteria for abandoning or demolishing the old and replacing it with the latest and most advanced material or device developed by our technological capacities. The thirst for newness became a cult, a throw-away economy replaced a concern for tradition and respect for heritage; individualism was replaced by the "man in the grey flannel suit." But society is resilient. And in the later 1970s and early 1980s, individualism returned, bringing with it nostalgia for the old, increased perception of historical values and an appreciation of the contribution of the individual.

In the 1980s, a sophisticated experimentation with classical symbols and decoration was known popularly as Post-Modernism. It was a period of unusual freedom of choice for the architect. Certainly, a principal goal of the Post-Modernist movement was to join with society in general in the search for institutions that provide a better balance between technology, resources, and the rights and responsibilities of the individual. Part of the increased formal variety was made possible by computer technology in the design process and in industry. Our global economy also has increased access to products and craftmanship.

Since the beginning of the Industrial Revolution, technical achievements have tended to develop more rapidly than other cultural concepts; society has constantly sought a better balance between technology and popular culture. Now that society is demanding a better balance, and our automated work world promises us more time to devote to social, moral, ethical, and political pursuits, we may be approaching the time when achievements in nontechnical concepts will match technical achievements. If so, the level of architectural taste demanded by our contemporary culture will be at once gratifying and challenging to the architectural profession. The promise of such balance is closer to achievement than it has been for generations. Your generation may see it accomplished.

THE CONSTRUCTION INDUSTRY

In the mid-1970s, it was estimated that the annual construction market in the United States totalled over 100 billion dollars, roughly $500.00 for each person in an estimated national population of 215 million. In November of 1991, the Department of Commerce reported that spending on new construction reached over 470 billion annually. Of this amount, the Department estimates that 370 billion is invested annually in private construction and over 100 billion annually in public agency construction including highways, military facilities, schools, and infrastructure systems such as sewers and water systems. Of the total amount of 470 billion dollars, 148 billion is spent annually on residential construction.

As we approach the mid-1990s, the economy is regaining its vigor. While new construction is down, the rehabilitation industry has improved thanks to an increased interest in the preservation of our older buildings and retention of existing stock as opposed to its demolition, clearance, and replacement. Technological advancements in communications and information exchange and in environmental control prompt more frequent retrofitting of building systems. The interior design market has expanded. Improved health systems and retirement programs are producing a much more economically vigorous health care industry and an increasing senior citizen population. Public building programs as diverse as prisons and schools have increased building regionally in our country. These trends all indicate increasing activity for the construction industry.

Construction is a cyclical industry, meaning it reflects fluctuations in the national economy sensitively and rapidly. During economic recessions, construction is often put off; whereas, in times of economic growth, the industry may find it difficult to keep up with the demand for its product. Since construction is so important to our economy, all levels of government have developed policies on the construction of public works in an attempt to minimize economic fluctuations. Extensive public construction projects are often undertaken in times of recession to stimulate a lagging economy.

Many other elements of the American economy join with the construction industry in building and maintaining our physical environment. Your school, for instance, contains thousands of separate products supplied by many different sources. Each product was conceived, designed, manufactured, shipped, and assembled through the employment of labor, materials, and capital supplied by various elements of our economy. To these activities must be added those required for daily servicing, maintaining, and repairing your school if we are to identify all those elements of our national economy which participate in the creation and maintenance of this single piece of your physical environment.

The many vocations included in the construction element of our national economy can be grouped into three general classifications:

The Design Group. Architects, engineers, and other professionals and technicians who design our physical environment.

The Constructor Group. Contractors, suppliers, manufacturers, and building trades who construct our physical environment.

The Support Group. Financiers, realtors, educators, insurance underwriters, testers and researchers, public administrators, and others who supply land, loan money, train personnel, and perform other services ancillary to the creation of our physical environment.

While a common thread of interest—construction—runs through all three groups and touches each person involved, there are considerable differences in individual motivations that lead each person to a particular type of work within the industry.

The Design Group

The design group includes people who have a basic interest in conceiving, programming, synthesizing, and planning our physical environment. These are personalities that think "in-the-round." They can visualize the effects of various relationships in space, color, texture, warmth, and light without first having to see, feel, or otherwise experience them. Characteristically, these are highly skilled and trained people with refined senses for what is appropriate to particular types of environments and functions. Typically, people in this group regard themselves as professionals—placing service to society and their profession above any personal gain.

The Constructor Group

Those in the constructor group are people of action. They want to experience the construction process firsthand, to work directly with the machines and materials used in the building process, and to see the building rise as a direct result of their effort. Many are businesspeople—contractors, suppliers, manufacturers—who, through astute management of personnel and machines, earn substantial monetary rewards in their various vocations.

The Support Group

The motivations and interests of those in the support group are as varied as the list of professions would indicate. The trades in this group render many vital services to the construction industry and, in turn, look to construction for a large share of their daily endeavors. Frequently, they must be as knowledgeable of the workings of the construction industry as are designers and constructors, and may well have gained their education or started their careers in those fields.

This summary of construction industry prospects and of the vocations encompassed within the industry gives you an idea of the breadth and potential of career opportunities it offers. You should particularly note that those who choose a career in design are at the heart of the industry—their decisions put other elements of the industry into action. Consequently, those trained in architecture find their careers can carry them throughout the industry—into engineering, construction, finance, manufacturing, public administration—as well as into design.

CONSTRUCTING A HIGH SCHOOL

To illustrate the broad potential of those trained and experienced in architecture, let us consider the design and construction of a high school.

Planning

To start the process, the board of education and the superintendent determine that a new school building is required. Their decision is based upon the need for more space to accommodate a growing student population, or perhaps an existing school needed replacement. In either event, architectural services are required to help them decide where to locate the school, what facilities to include, and its approximate cost. An architect in private practice is retained to make studies on location, function, and cost and to assist the school board and the administration in making their decision. The private practice of architecture engages by far the greatest number of architects in the United States. It offers the opportunity to own and operate your own business and professional enterprise and to share in all the challenges and rewards of being your own boss and directing your own affairs.

Public agencies, such as your school district, often employ architects on their administrative staffs who perform in-house architectural services on buildings that house agency functions, They also work with architects in private practice when the agency undertakes major building projects. Such public agency positions offer rewarding careers to those architects attracted to public service.

In making studies on location, the architect working for the school district consults with local city planning commissions on plans for neighborhood development. These plans are a matter of urban design in which architects have participated, as members of the planning commission, employees of the commission's staff, or private planning consultants. Urban planning is a challenging field for those trained in architecture. Architects with special interests in urban design, geography, sociology, economics, or public administration have many career opportunities either as private consultants or as staff members of federal, state, and local agencies concerned with urban development.

As the architect and the school board study the functions and activities to be included in your school building, they call in special consultants on various educational planning problems, such as television and team teaching, visual aids, and auditorium and stage design. Some architects in private practice specialize in particular kinds of buildings; for instance, schools, theaters, hospitals, or shopping centers. Others specialize in particular functions within a building, such as kitchen and cafeteria areas, hospital operating suites, or X-ray and radiology rooms. As a building-type consultant, an architect has an opportunity to concentrate on those areas of the construction industry he or she finds of greatest interest.

To develop cost figures for constructing and maintaining the school building through the issuance of bonds, the school board and the architect consult with taxing and bonding authorities expert in the field of construction financing. Construction requires loan money; that is, money loaned to the owner of the building—in this case your school board—by commercial institutions, such as banks and insurance companies whose business it is to supply money. Such lending institutions offer unusual career opportunities for architects with particular interests in construction economics and finance. Further, many such institutions deal principally with public construction that is financed through tax and bond revenues. These institutions offer additional career openings for architects knowledgeable in public finance and tax administration.

Having determined that the school should be built, the school board directs the architect to prepare detailed drawings and specifications for the construction of the building. The architect then brings together and directs a team of professionals and technicians skilled in the many disciplines required in building design and construction. Most of these talents are members of the architect's staff. For certain specialized areas of design, the architect retains other private consultants to assist in the preparation of the drawings and specifications. The design of contemporary buildings requires architectural designers, structural engineers, mechanical engineers, specification writers, interior designers, planners for special equipment, draftsmen, and a host of special supporting talents, such as computer programmers, statisticians, technical writers, systems analysts, researchers, business administrators, and estimators. Those trained in architecture can be specialized in any of these fields, depending upon their desires, talents, and special education.

Members of the design team call in a number of materials and building systems experts—often representatives or salespeople from various building product manufacturers—requesting information and recommendations on the use and limitations of hundreds of different products considered during the design process. The sophisticated technology of present-day building materials requires manufacturer's representatives to be educated and trained in technology and research as well as in sales. Architects whose special talents lie in product design and development, or in sales, will find many career opportunities with manufacturers.

The architect checks the drawings and specifications as they were developed with federal, state, and local public agencies to determine that the building design conforms to code. Public agencies responsible for the administration of building codes and other regulations affecting construction offer rewarding careers for architects interested in public health and safety.

As the detailed drawings and specifications are completed, they are combined with insurance and legal documents developed by attorneys and insurance underwriters retained by the school board. The legal, insurance, and bonding elements of the construction industry afford many career openings for those trained in architecture who also have an interest in finance or law.

The drawings, specifications, and related construction contract documents are completed, and building contractors are invited to review them carefully, estimate the cost of the labor and materials involved, and then submit a bid for constructing the school. This bidding process takes about thirty days, and during this period, each of the contractors call upon many other persons to help complete the estimates.

Suppliers are asked to estimate the cost of furnishing and delivering concrete, brick, pipe, wire, and many other materials that the contractor's own workers would put together at the site. Manufacturers are contacted to estimate the cost of those parts of the building which are to be factory-fabricated and shipped to the school site ready for installation. Subcontractors estimate the cost of those portions of the construction work that the contractor expects to assign to them.

The contractor goes through every detail in the documents, mentally constructing the building; determining the construction technique required; planning the use of equipment; checking each estimate received from suppliers, manufacturers, and subcontractors; and coordinating and scheduling all phases of the work so that the school will be completed efficiently, expeditiously, and economically. Construction management—the scheduling of construction work, estimating and controlling its cost, and coordinating its many separate operations—is of vital importance to the construction industry. Historically, construction managers have risen throughout the ranks of the constructors. With the increasing complexity of building design and the advent of computerized scheduling and costing techniques, there is an ever-growing demand in construction management for architects and engineers having that unique combination of talents—design plus management plus administration skills.

Construction

When the contractors complete their estimates, each submits a bid to the school board and the architect. A construction contract is signed between the board and the contractor submitting the lowest dollar bid, and the construction begins.

Construction of your school will probably take from ten to eighteen months, depending upon the project's size. During construction, countless decisions are made as to construction methods, materials, and techniques required to produce the result called for in the contract documents. The architect and consultants participate in this process by providing important interpretations and clarifications of the documents as they were requested by the contractor. Just as important are the interpretations of the architect's intent that are rendered by the contractor and by hundreds of other persons responsible for producing the parts of the finished school. Subcontractors, manufacturers and suppliers, testing and inspecting agencies, insurance and bonding agents, financing sources, and the school board itself participated in this ongoing decision-making process. Building construction provides many rewarding opportunities for the construction technician—those architects with special expertise in construction superintendence, drafting, testing and inspection, factory production of component parts or similar services contributing to the construction of a building through the interpretation of architectural drawings and specifications.

As construction progresses, the public improvements required to service the school—roads, sanitary and storm drainage, water and utility lines are constructed by appropriate public agencies. Although such improvements are not actually a part of the building project, they are made necessary by it, and their design and construction must be coordinated with that of the school. The design and construction of public improvements by federal, state and local agencies, and by private utilities offer rewarding career opportunities for architects who wish to devote their talents to a public service career.

The Finishing Touches

Site improvements and landscaping are then undertaken. Athletic fields and courts, playground equipment, access roads and parking lots, walks, fencing, lighting, sodding, and plantings are placed, and the school begins to look like a permanent part of the community. Landscape design, site planning, and construction demand a unique kind of architectural talent—a combination of building design, landscape architecture, civil engineering, and urban design.

Interior finish, furnishings, and equipment are completed next. Furniture, rugs, draperies, library shelving, cafeteria equipment, auditorium seating, stage lighting and curtains, science tables, gymnasium equipment, and hundreds of other finish and equipment items are installed. Interior design, including design of special service equipment, graphics, and signage, offers interesting and varied careers to architects who wish to focus their talents on creating harmonious, stimulating, and serviceable interior environments.

The school is complete. As a significant statement of its time and community, it is of interest to other people and other communities. Press releases are sent to local and national news media representatives, some of whom visit the completed school to gather additional information for dissemination through radio, TV, magazines, and newspapers.

Architectural journalism and architectural photography, including architectural criticism and real estate commentary, are inviting fields for those trained in architecture who find they have complementary talents in writing or photography. In this age of communication and interpretation, such talents are in great demand.

Maintenance

Following the school's completion, continuing maintenance and repair, and perhaps remodeling, will be needed to adapt the school to changing educational demands. Such post-completion programs, if not responsive to the building design's original intent, can drastically restrict its successful operation. Professional services in building maintenance, repair, and remodeling afford unusual opportunities to architects who seek a career combining design with performance evaluation testing, research, and development.

The cycle of activities begun by the decision to build a new school is completed years later when the school board makes arrangements for the abandonment and sale of the existing school facilities. They announce the intended sale of the building and call for purchase bids from interested developers. Chances are that the school has become a community landmark. People interested in its preservation as a landmark speak out and ask that the building not be demolished, that it be somehow retained as essential to the historical record of the community's culture and growth.

Historic preservation is a field of growing interest to architects and one that promises increased opportunities for career pursuit. The historic preservationist must have a comprehensive knowledge of historic architectural styles and the contribution of these styles to a community's artistic and historic environment. As important, however, is the ability of the historic preservationist to suggest and document adaptive uses that might be made of valued buildings that have outlived their original functional purpose. This requires a talent for putting together packages of uses and ownership arrangements that make it economically feasible to retain the building for some other use while retaining the integrity of those features of the building that make it a landmark. Finally, the preservationist must be intimately knowledgeable of craftsmanship and construction techniques required for authentic rehabilitation of older buildings.

From the late 1970s, more and more educational facilities were being abandoned due to the drop in school-age population. This trend is predicted to continue well into the 1990s. At the same time the need for housing for the elderly and for additional community service facilities such as counseling centers and neighborhood health centers has been increasing. Such a use may have been made of your former school building through a developmental package assembled by architects, contractors, and financiers for just such a purpose.

This brief discussion of the design, construction, and maintenance of a school and the recycling of its older facilities is a practical illustration of the broad range of career opportunities offered by the construction industry and open to those with basic training and experience in architecture. You can see that architecture, while basically a matter of environmental design, prepares students for entrance into countless other disciplines. Indeed, this broad career potential is a prime advantage to those trained and experienced in architecture.

THE ENVIRONMENTAL DESIGN PROFESSIONS

Today the construction industry, with the leadership of the environmental design professions—architecture, engineering, landscape architecture, and urban planning—has the technical resources to enclose and control the climate of an entire urban area within a single structure. You know of large shopping centers, stadiums, and other big building complexes throughout the United States that point to this possibility of completely enclosing and controlling a defined area of our physical environment. You also know of the rapid advancements being made in ground, water, and air transport facilities to service our physical environment. Further, you recognize the increasing attention being given to the remaking of existing urban areas and to the preservation and enhancement of our nation's natural resources—its open spaces, wilderness areas, water and air resources.

All these activities involve the services of those trained and experienced in the environmental design professions. If we are to rebuild a good share of our existing development and preserve our remaining natural resources, it is easy to see that environmental designers have an immense task ahead of them. The career opportunities are commensurate with this great challenge.

Those directly involved in the design and construction of our environment are not the only members of the environmental design profession. As in every other vocation, the art and science of environmental design requires the services of those who teach its disciplines to others who search out and record and interpret its activities to society. Thus, these professions include many career opportunities for those whose basic training is in design but who wish to devote their talents to design education, archaeology, construction science, technical writing, or other fields that combine a background in design with a unique talent in a second discipline. Your future might well be in one of these combined careers.

To illustrate the broad range of career opportunities open to those who choose to enter the environmental design professions, we can make a simple checklist of some of the disciplines included in or related to these professions. In reviewing this list, you should note again that architecture is the basic art and science of the environmental design professions; that those trained in architecture therefore have the broadest choice of career opportunities in the design of our physical environment.

Disciplines within Environmental Design

Primary Disciplines

Architecture
Engineering
Landscape Architecture
Planning

Component and Related Disciplines

Analysis	Economic and Market Potential
	Land Use and Feasibility
Programming	Functional Relationships and Space Utilization
Promotion	Job Development
	Real Estate Assembly
	Land and Construction Scheduling
Design	Area and Space Planning
	Urban Design, Transportation, Utilities, and Site Planning
	Structural, Mechanical, Electrical, Sanitary, Acoustical, Vibration, and similar engineering design
	Drafting, Specification Writing, Product Analysis
	Interiors and Equipment Planning
	Fine Arts and Graphics Planning
Financing	Cost Estimating and Analysis
	Construction Cost Accounting
Construction	Bidding and Contract Negotiation
	Contract Administration
	Construction Management
	Maintenance and Repair

Supporting   Archaeology and Preservation
              Construction Law
              Insurance and Sureties
              Research and Testing
              Product Development and Fabrication
              Education
              Reporting and Criticism
              Photography, Model Making, and
                  Presentations

CAREER OPTIONS

Those trained and experienced in architecture have a variety of career options available to them. One may choose to pursue one of these alternative careers after investing a few years in the profession and finding that a personal interest in one facet of the design and construction process has developed into an expertise recognized by others and requiring full-time attention to refine. Or, one may switch careers after having mastered the conventional practice of architecture. Here are five such alternative careers that have proven rewarding to many architects who have chosen to pursue them.

Preservation and Rehabilitation

The study of the history of architecture is a basic interest of those drawn to the fields of architecture and other elements of environmental design. Courses in architectural history comprise a significant portion of the architect's education. For most architects, an interest in the roots of the art and science of architecture continues throughout their career. This interest is shared with the general public. For instance, a fair share of the recreation and tourism business is based upon a general popular fascination with our heritage and the lifestyles of our ancestors. If you were to vacation in Europe, for example, your itinerary would almost certainly focus on visiting structures and places important to the development of our Western culture. In this country, we have long given special recognition to places such as Mount Vernon and Monticello that are associated with our nation's early leaders.

In recent years the growing popular interest in knowing more about and conserving our heritage has extended our concern for preserving more and more of our existing structures. Young families are interested in fixing up older homes, and businesses frequently look for the opportunity to rehabilitate existing commercial structures. Public officials view the adaptive reuse of our older structures as an option equal to tearing down that structure and replacing it with a new facility. Federal, state, and local organizations devoted to preserving structures and districts have become important political forces in the establishment of public policy.

The movement in historic preservation and rehabilitation can take the form of saving entire blocks or districts as well as individual buildings. Further, the movement extends to all building types, from individual residences and commercial buildings to entire neighborhoods in urban areas. The interest may involve landmark structures of importance to our cultural heritage because of some person or event associated with that structure. It can also simply encompass a building or neighborhood having a special unity of design within a larger, mixed urban setting.

The saving and rehabilitation of these structures and districts has now become a significant career opportunity for architects. Rehabilitation work requires structural and other feasibility studies to determine the cost and time requirements of saving the structures and to find an adaptive use that may be placed in the rehabilitated facility. Most recently, changes in the tax legislation, building code requirements, and funding assistance have made investment in rehabilitation activities more attractive.

As a result of this growing interest in historic preservation, increasing numbers of public and private agencies and of architectural firms are devoted to serving this interest. Consequently, many students and practitioners are devoting portions of their careers to preservation. Given the recent renewed awareness of our cultural heritage and our concern for conservation of resources, it seems certain that preservation and rehabilitation services offered by the environmental design professions will continue to provide significant career opportunities.

Construction Management and Development

Construction management is a relatively new discipline within environmental design. It arises from the need to provide greater overall coordination to the design and construction processes from the beginning of programming through the completion of construction and the occupancy of the facility.

Construction management firms are frequently retained directly by an owner to advise and consult on the programming, design, and cost-estimating activities of the architect and to coordinate the work schedules, material deliveries, and trade jurisdiction of the various contractors. The objective of such services is to effect cost savings in the ways that elements of the building process are brought together and to reduce the length of time the project takes from conception to completion. Those who find their talents and interests taking them into construction techniques, cost-estimating procedures, and the business management aspects of construction are finding construction management an attractive career option. Building owners and investors find construction management services attractive because they provide professional counsel throughout the entire design/construction process. The owner and his or her financial partners can save considerable time in major building projects by using the construction management system.

City and Regional Planning

City planning and building is an ancient art. Among its earliest practitioners were the Romans who, in building military outposts to support their expanding empire, laid out a number of new cities with considerable precision. The sites of many of these new communities became, in later times, major European centers. European colonists, particularly the Spanish and, in some cases, the English, came to North America with well-developed ideas on how the various parts of a city should be laid out. Many South American capitals, for instance, display the influence of the initial city plans laid out by the church and military officials accompanying the early Spanish explorers. In our own country, Philadelphia, Washington, D.C., and Savannah, Georgia, are examples of English and French influences on early city planning and building. During the Industrial Revolution, little attention was given to the art of building cities. Urban concentration extended across the landscape as a result of the real estate industry's skill at dividing up and selling off the land as rapidly as possible. The unrelieved grid patterns of many American cities west of the Alleghenies show this trend.

In the late 1800s, interest in city planning suddenly revived. A number of major American cities developed extensive plans for remodeling and beautification of their central areas. Today, in cities such as Chicago, St. Louis, Denver, Cleveland, and San Francisco, this interest is evidenced in extensive parks, open space, and rather formal public buildings in their central areas. Much of this planning was the work of a small group of people frequently led by Daniel Burnham, a Chicago architect.

From the 1920s through the 1940s, growing interest in city and regional planning extended to increased zoning codes, subdivision regulations and other controls placed upon the use and development of land. Following World War II, rapid population growth and increased use of automobiles resulted in a sudden need for more housing, schools, shopping centers, highways, industrial parks, airports, and other facilities. There was great concern that these facilities be adequately serviced by utilities and that they be properly related to one another. This concern gave rise to increasing interest in environmental pollution and conservation issues brought about by postwar construction.

Out of all this activity came the development and recognition of the city and regional planning profession with all its disciplines, ranging from resource planning and physical design, through urban sociology and economics, to political science and public management. Today, the planning profession offers varied and attractive career options to those trained and experienced in architecture. Many students who have completed their first degree in architecture choose to take advanced work in urban planning. Others find their first employment in public or private planning offices, which feature programs in urban design. The architect in private practice frequently contributes to city planning to some degree in order to better fit a building project into its neighborhood.

Given our increasing concern for the proper use of land-based resources, there can be little doubt that the planning profession will continue to offer many career opportunities to architects interested in urban design. These professions can be pursued in private practice or in public agencies. The architect/urban designer/city planner in the public agency will most likely find development of broad public policy to be the principal assignment. In private practice, this same person will find the principal work to be support of the public policy through the design and construction of a particular project. Thus, there is a choice between approaches to utilizing a wide range of talents and interests.

In the last few years, yet another new and unique combination of architectural/city planning/urban design/construction career opportunities has emerged and is being refined into a new discipline within the environmental design construction field. One might refer to this new discipline as "city rebuilder." Individuals and private firms who practice this discipline contract with municipalities to rebuild significant portions of the municipality. Work recently completed in and around the Baltimore Inner Harbor area is an example. Similar work has been completed in the Boston waterfront area and is proposed for the Navy Pier facility in Chicago. To date, these activities have concentrated on "people places," i.e. those areas of a city that have certain historic features that, if rehabilitated, promise to draw large numbers of visitors seeking relaxation and entertainment. Nearly every city in the United States is now considering a project or two that would repeat the success of the Baltimore and Boston undertakings. They have brought a whole new level of ambiance to the centers of those cities. These successes are producing private firms that specialize in the rehabilitation of the older parts of our cities. They bring a very high level of organizational talent, design sensitivity, and construction expertise to the client community, thereby relieving that community of the need for such on-staff talent. Their organizational talents include expertise in public and private financing and thorough knowledge of the many local, state, and federal regulations governing the design and construction of public facilities.

These organizations are now turning their attention to the rehabilitation of the more commonplace retail, office, and industrial portions of our cities, and the opportunities for the architect/urban designer/city planner are increasing.

Part of this growth in the city rebuilding field may be traced to our general recognition that our resources are limited and must be conserved. This suggests that our older cities should be rehabilitated as opposed to being abandoned in favor of new development on the edge of the city. Our renewed interest in our community's heritage is also part of the reason.

Communications

Communications are important in all human endeavors. In the service industries and in the professions, where interpersonal relationships are basic to the provision of services to the buyer, communications are critical. In the environmental design professions, communications usually take the form of drawings or other fixed graphics, and written text to cover those items not treated in the graphics. Thus, the architect's sketches, formal perspectives, working drawings, specifications and various contract forms are developed by the architect for communications with clients, contractors, subcontractors, and others essential to the design and construction process.

But an architect's communications do not begin or end with drawn and written materials. The architect must also develop verbal talents necessary for gaining approval of the designs developed in response to clients' needs. The architect's communications range across all available tools and techniques of exchanging information with those involved in the building process.

After some years of experience, an architect may find that he or she possesses a special talent—verbal, textual, or graphic—in the field of communications, and will gain increasing recognition for those particular talents and abilities. In essence, that talent will be recognized as a particular ability to reduce a problem to its essentials, to organize the solution to that problem, and to clearly explain the solution to others. As this talent grows and is broadly recognized, the architect will be increasingly called upon as a communicator and will develop special techniques specially suited to her or his particular type of practice, audience, and personal sense of what tools he or she works best with—written, drawn, or spoken; print, graphic, film, or electronic media.

This increasing sophistication and growing expertise may well lead the architect into a full-time career in journalism, lecturing, teaching, film, television, graphic arts, or another facet of the communications industry.

This does not mean that the architect must necessarily leave the field of architecture in order to pursue this developing talent in communications. In larger environmental design offices, the architect may well find those talents devoted to the work of the firm—the promotion of services, the preparation of project reports, or the representation of the firm and the profession before the public. On the other hand, the architect with such skills may find career opportunities within the communications industries to be more attractive, and may consider a switch of careers from architecture to communications.

Professional Associations

Professional and public interest associations are traditional American institutions. Chances are that you belong to one or more such groups. Examples might be a conservation society, a local youth association, the YMCA, YWCA, JCC, a debate club, or similar group. Most likely you know adults who have long been members of a trade, professional, political, or specialized citizen group that expresses their interest in a particular subject on a local, state, or national level.

In the years since World War II, the number of nonprofit associations has grown immensely throughout the United States. This growth is the result of our increasing awareness of the need to take part in the shaping of public attitudes and subsequent programs affecting our working and living environments and our general quality of life. Many of these organizations offer attractive career opportunities for those trained in environmental design, and it is common for an architect, sometime during his or her career development, to be on the staff of such an organization.

A review of the yellow pages of a telephone directory in any major American city will reveal a considerable number of such associations. Washington, D.C., of course, has thousands since one of the principal purposes of such groups is to influence legislation. Similarly, most state capitals, or the major urban areas within each state, have a number of similar institutions.

While there are many large nationwide associations that can support a headquarters staff of several dozen professionals and technicians, there is a much larger number of local groups with several hundred members and a staff of only a few people. Typically, these groups depend upon membership dues, foundation grants, and special purpose study and research project funding for their financial bases. Their activities involve writing proposals for legislation, advocacy and lobbying before appropriate elected and appointed bodies, sponsorship of debate on public policy issues, public education programs, execution of research programs, and fund-raising to support all these varied activities.

The interests of these groups may range from the joining together of local professionals for the betterment of their own disciplines; to groups that sponsor improved local planning and housing programs; to regional and state organizations promoting the understanding of open space needs, historic preservation techniques, and similar environmental issues; and to national organizations of professional and citizen groups interested in environmental or other issues at the federal level. All these organizations require trained professional staff to execute programs responsive to the organization's interest. Obviously, a trained architect is often essential.

A staff job with one of these associations may be a part-time student position, a summer position, a graduate intern position, or a career association executiveship. Washington, D.C., for instance, has many trained and experienced design professionals who have devoted the bulk of their careers to employment in professional associations. Salaries, benefits, and related work environments for the association executive are equivalent to those found in private firms and public agencies. A particular satisfaction of such a career is the contributions one can make linking public and private interest for the betterment of environmental design.

NEED FOR PERSONNEL

In the post-World War II period, from the late 1940s to the mid-1970s, there were not enough practitioners to fill existing positions within the design professions. With the economic recession of the mid-1970s, this situation changed. The schools that had attracted increasing numbers of students over the postwar years began to produce more graduates than the design professions could absorb. Consequently, many professionals left design practice and entered other fields to stay employed. Others expanded their practice activities to include development and construction of their own investment projects. All in all, this shake-out period proved most beneficial. It introduced new career potentials to many individuals who found that their new careers were more suited to their talents. It also caused many of those who continued traditional private practice to step back and refine their design skills.

Still, it was a difficult time for recent graduates. Jobs were scarce. Many graduates found themselves returning to school for further education, or traveling to broaden their perception and understanding of the art and science of architecture. Others simply took what they considered to be temporary jobs in other areas to wait for an opportunity to enter, full-time, into their chosen profession. Again, all in all, this was a fortuitous development. It tended to disperse design talents through a broad spectrum of our business and cultural community. This may well pay substantial dividends in the future as these design-trained individuals move up to decision-making positions in the everyday business world.

In the latter 1970s, the construction industry seemed to have regained some of its earlier energy and momentum. The recession period that began in late 1979 and worsened in early 1980 brought another slowdown. This cyclical pattern is always indicative of the nation's general economic health. To be sure, the nature of building activity will continue to change. There will probably be less emphasis on new construction and greater emphasis on redevelopment, rehabilitation, and revitalization. More attention will be given to conservation, rather than exploitation, of our resources. More energies will be devoted to studying a problem and developing alternative solutions than to racing ahead with a solution that simply overwhelms the problem. These more reasoned approaches to problem solving will require greater and more refined talents than those required by our earlier, grosser techniques. It is also to be hoped that the design solutions reached will be more surely recommended and more rewarding to their developers.

Our society will continue to seek well-trained and dedicated design talent. Graduates in architecture, engineering, landscape architecture, and urban planning should continue to find adequate career openings in their chosen profession. The actual demand for personnel within each profession will vary from year to year and from region to region. The vagaries of population growth, regional shifts due to climatic and resource pressure, individual mobility, and simple personal preferences as to choice of life-style and environment play a very dynamic part in our nation's economic profile. You are a part of this profile, and where you choose to live and work contributes to the various statistics that you analyze in making that choice. Your choice, in turn, influences new federal, state, and local programs for urban revitalization, the creation of open space, the design and construction of transportation systems, the use and conservation of natural resources, and the development of countless programs in nations outside of our own country. All these activities add to the demand for design professionals.

There is little question that our colleges and universities can produce enough graduate design professionals to fill the demand. Some observers maintain that the schools are producing more graduates than the profession can absorb. While this may be true of the design professions as narrowly defined in the historic sense, it is certainly not the case if the graduate views career opportunities in the broad sense advocated in this book. The employment outlook is always better for graduates who are flexible and who are openly willing to consider any opportunity to apply their talents, wherever that opportunity may arise.

AUTOMATION

What effect will automation have on career opportunities in the design professions? Automation will increase rather than decrease total career opportunities in the design professions. Computerization of design functions—structural analysis, for instance—relieves the professional of the detail work formerly required in solving all sorts of design problems. It allows more time for the productive, creative work that no machine can do. To be sure, automation will have a dramatic effect on the details of individual jobs—the drafter, for instance, will gradually evolve into a specially trained computer programmer or computer graphics technician.

In the long run, automation will be of great assistance to the construction industry; it helps increase productivity in what is a very labor-intensive field. Labor-intensive industries are very sensitive to inflationary pressures and, in this age of governmental regulation, these pressures have increased because of various governmental restrictions. For instance, today the design professions and their construction associates are very concerned about land use, environmental impacts, resource allocation, and personnel policies. These concerns cost money, both in loss of productivity and in additional social cost. While automation cannot in itself relieve these pressures, it can assist the industry in responding to them and thus lower costs while increasing the industry's productivity. In fact, these results may prove to be the most beneficial of all consequences of automation.

AGE LIMITATIONS

There are no age limitations that are peculiar to the design professions as a discipline. Experience, as well as education, is a desirable characteristic of any endeavor. The usual professional does not reach peak earning or professional capacity until 45 to 55 years of age. As for retirement, architects usually remain active for as many years as ability, stamina, and desire indicate. It is also characteristic for the designer/architect to remain active in the community's social, cultural, political and/or academic circles long after retirement from an active business career.

OPPORTUNITIES FOR WOMEN

Until the 1970s, the status of women in the environmental design profession and the construction industry was little different than it was elsewhere in American business and industry. Generally speaking, opportunities for education in the professions were limited, and job openings were scarce. Once having found employment, women found that their incomes were considerably lower than those of male colleagues. Women's hourly rates were lower, and they received "unequal pay for equal work."

This situation has been largely turned around. By the early 1970s, women architects began to form organizations within the profession to examine the work environments and professional advancement available to women. In 1973, men and women members of The American Institute of Architects (AIA) brought their concerns to the attention of the general membership. This resulted in a study on the status of women in architecture. Existing employment practices were reviewed and subsequently acted upon to integrate women in all aspects of the profession as full participants. In 1974, a study committee within the AIA surveyed this situation and produced a landmark finding on the subject of women and ethnic minorities in the field of architecture. As a result, the AIA has been devoted to the development and promotion of long-range affirmative action programs for correcting discrimination in the profession.

These programs have produced some results, although there remains a vast difference between the number of women involved in the profession as compared to the number of men. Current estimates indicate that less than 10 percent of all the architects in the United States are women. As of the end of 1991, 9.1% of all AIA members were women. Most of those women are engaged in design rather than construction. Their activities include programming, interiors, graphics, space planning, and similar in-house work. Increasingly, however, women are encouraged to consider careers in structural, electrical, and mechanical engineering, construction estimating, and firm management.

At the same time, it is wise to remember that there have always been opportunities for women in the design profession, particularly in such disciplines as urban and regional planning, interior design, and landscape architecture. One difference between yesterday and today is that salary structures, benefits, advancement potential, and other components of the work environments have been made equal to those available to men. In the last few years women architects have made some progress with salary and career growth. Other future changes in the demography of the profession depend primarily on the numbers of men and women entering the profession and upon the talents of those individuals.

EARNINGS

Income levels depend on several factors—population densities, geography, local economies, and working patterns. Salaries for professionals will generally be higher in urban areas than in rural, but living expenses will also be higher.

Just as in other fields, earnings in the design professions are usually greater in private practice than in public employment, but public employment often provides the professional with greater opportunity to influence thinking in the field. This is especially true of urban and regional planning and of some fields of environmental planning. Obviously, income is only one employment consideration, and fringe benefits, cost-of-living, position, and job satisfaction must also be weighed to determine attractiveness of a particular profession.

A steadily rising standard of living and an uncertain economy complicate the income picture. Beginning annual salaries in the design professions have risen from $8,000 in 1970 to $24,000 in 1990, and the average principal's salary has risen from $25,000–$30,000 to $67,000 during the same period of time.

In spite of all these factors, we can cite a few rules of thumb about the earning and work patterns of the design professions that hold true over the years:

Earnings are generally higher in private practice than in public employment.

There is a paid internship—that is, the graduate makes a living wage immediately upon entering practice.

Earnings fall into the median of all professionals, i.e., below doctors and dentists, about the same as lawyers and accountants.

Incomes over $100,000, are rare.

A typical job encompasses a wide variety of tasks in a wide range of situations.

There is a great deal of geographic and job mobility because of personnel shortages.

Construction is a cyclical industry, and incomes can vary according to local building activity.

Deadlines are commonplace, often requiring overtime and evening work.

Your clients must live with your work for a long time—both successes and failures.

EDUCATIONAL REQUIREMENTS

A later chapter details the educational requirements for architecture, but we will take a moment here to comment on what is happening generally in education for the design professions.

In the past, architects, engineers, and landscape architects completed their university training in four or five years. Advanced degrees have always been available, but the usual professional graduate entered practice after earning a Bachelor of Arts (B.A.) degree. Urban planners, on the other hand, have characteristically entered practice after earning a Master of Arts (M.A.) degree, based upon a B.A. in architecture, engineering, or some other related discipline plus the required graduate work of one to two years. In recent years, more and more students in all disciplines have been earning advanced degrees. In some cases universities have dropped their undergraduate professional degrees and now expect students to go on to graduate work if they expect to become qualified professionals.

The design professions are upgrading their educational qualifications in response to the demand for more highly trained graduates. Should you consider an advanced degree? The answer is almost certainly "yes" if you seek to develop every skill and talent available to you in building your career. The advanced degree is becoming as common as the B.A. was previously. As always, those with the best qualifications will advance the most rapidly.

LICENSING

Most professionals in the United States are licensed to practice their profession. The candidates must pass an examination given by the state of residence before they can practice medicine, law, architecture, or engineering. In most cases, these examinations are given some time after the individual has graduated, during which time he or she serves an internship in actual professional practice under the guidance of a licensed practitioner.

In the case of the design professions, the requirements for licensing vary. Architects and engineers are required to be licensed in every state, landscape architects in about one third of the states, and urban planners, in two states. In any event, the chances are that if you choose to enter the design professions, you must plan on a period of internship followed by a licensing examination before qualifying as a professional.

CAREER CHOICE AND CAREER OPPORTUNITY

You now realize that if you choose a career in architecture, you really choose a career in creating our physical environment. With architectural training you will have the best possible qualifications to move throughout the entire sphere of the construction industry and the design professions. And as an architect, your career potential is essentially a matter of choosing among many kinds of challenging opportunities.

CHAPTER 2

THE PROFESSIONAL ARCHITECT

By reading this book, you are preparing yourself to choose a vocation. A vocation is a regular occupation or profession, specifically, one for which you are especially suited or qualified.

When you choose a particular kind of work, you are selecting a part of the business world that you find attractive and feel would offer the best opportunity for the gainful employment of your unique talents. You are choosing an occupation. For some people, this first choice is sufficient and they follow their chosen occupation for 40–50 productive years, developing their talents to a fine degree and marketing them for satisfying monetary rewards. Indeed, the standard of living you presently enjoy as a citizen of the United States is largely the result of just such an application of talents.

For many other people, an occupation alone is not sufficient; they want to do more than simply work at a chosen occupation. Some people believe that, in carrying out everyday work activities, service to others becomes more important than personal recognition or the accumulation of wealth. You will find persons with this outlook in all walks of life: the farmers, for instance, who tend the soil so they leave it more productive than they found it; the administrator who insists upon excellence in working conditions as well as worker performance; the businessperson who not only markets a quality product but also backs its performance with a personal guarantee of service. Such persons have deep personal commitments to the well-being of humanity and believe strongly in their personal responsibility to serve this commitment.

This kind of personal outlook is a basic attitude required of those who enter theology, law, medicine, architecture, engineering, education, urban planning, and other disciplines devoted to the service of humanity. Such disciplines are called the professions. Their hallmark is basic concern for people—their health, safety, and general welfare. This ideal is popularly referred to as "protection of the public interest." An appreciation of the obligations and responsibilities attendant to this concern is essential to entering a profession. This chapter examines these obligations and responsibilities, because to properly discharge this commitment to the public interest, you will have to dedicate yourself to intensive study and practice throughout your formal education and your professional career.

THE PUBLIC INTEREST

All of us have a commitment to the protection of the public interest. That is, each of us as a citizen has a responsibility to uphold the law, to support our public institutions, and to conduct our personal affairs generally in a manner that does not injure our fellow citizens. As members of society, we develop rules of conduct, procedures for settling disputes, and methods for the organizing of our government. Collectively, these systems serve to protect our health, safety, and general welfare.

The professional's responsibility is not only to promote the observance of these laws and procedures as a citizen, but to apply them in daily practice, to interpret their intent for other citizens, defend their application where required, and suggest their modification by society when and where it seems appropriate. As you can appreciate, to exercise this responsibility properly, professionals must have an overriding interest in the welfare of people. For the doctor, this interest exhibits itself in a concern for the health and physical well-being of the community; for the lawyer, in a concern for law and justice equally applicable and available to all; for the architect, in a concern for a functional, safe, and pleasing physical environment.

But the professional does not act alone in discharging these responsibilities. The professional depends upon others—clients—to present problems that require the exercise of the professional's judgment based upon previous training and experience. This is how the professional earns a fee. Characteristically then, the professional stands somewhere between the client's interest and the public interest, and has a responsibility to see a way that both are served. This is not an easy task. It often requires that the professional frankly advise the client that the problem can't be solved without violating the public interest. Just as often, it will require that the professional vigorously defend the client's position and advocate a modification of a popularly held attitude or belief, or a change in the application of a public rule or regulation. Frequently, then, the professional will advise a client to take a certain action based upon moral and technical issues that may have little or nothing to do with the amount of the fee, or of the client's profit, or any other monetary issues involved.

REQUIREMENTS OF THE PROFESSION

To prepare for such a career, you will be required to undertake formal schooling ranging from five to seven years in an accredited professional school, serve an apprenticeship from one to three years after graduation, and pass an examination for licensure administered by your state of residence. Upon entering practice, you will be expected to uphold and defend both the rules and regulations established by the public to govern the practice of your profession and certain other codes of ethics or standards of practice developed by your peers to guide you in the exercise of your professional responsibilities.

Maintaining these rules and regulations will remain your responsibility throughout your professional career. Furthermore, the technical advancements and refinements in your field of interest after you graduate will undoubtedly require that you periodically return to the classroom for refresher courses in certain techniques. Indeed, depending on your special interests, you may return to school many times over several years of practice and thereby earn an advanced degree or two in highly specialized fields.

The demands made upon students and practitioners of any profession should not be minimized. The periods of study, internship, and licensure noted above are intensive, and similar burdens continue throughout the professional's career. Moreover, professional study is comparatively expensive, and the beginning income of many professionals is often below that of the average college graduate.

There are rewards also, of course, and they are intrinsic as well as material: the satisfaction of exercising personal independent judgment in solving another's problems; the joy of creating and successfully executing such solutions; the appreciation of clients and a public satisfactorily served; the recognition that results from professional success.

Knowing these demands and rewards, you should consider the following questions at this point in your search for a career.

Personal Character. Can you meet the high standards of character and conduct required of one who acts as a professional adviser?

Human Understanding. Do you have the patience and understanding to deal with people as their professional adviser?

Stamina and Discipline. Do you have the stamina to see yourself through years of intensive study and the sense of personal discipline to shape your professional growth all throughout your career?

Rewards. Are you willing to accept the intrinsic rather than material rewards characteristically associated with having a professional career?

If you can answer "yes" to each of these points, you have the basic attitudes required for the rigors of a professional career.

THE PROFESSION OF ARCHITECTURE

Architecture is for people, and the foremost purpose of any building is to provide functional, healthful, safe, and pleasing shelter for human activity. A building affects not only its occupants, but its period of history and all those who come into contact with it. If a building is to be successful, its design must be appropriate to its time in history, to its place in the community, and to its function as a shelter. Its construction must be economical, safe, and of sound, well-maintained materials. The architectural profession must advise the public and the construction industry in the production of buildings that answer these criteria, and the individual architect must design these buildings and administrate the contracts for their construction. By discharging these responsibilities in their day-to-day practices, the members of the architectural profession protect the public interest while creating our constructed physical environment.

Any profession so vitally concerned with the protection of the public interest will develop certain private organizations and public regulative devices to assist it in the advancement of the art and science of its profession. Thus architecture—like other recognized professions such as law, medicine, dentistry, and accounting—exhibits four organizational and regulative devices characteristic of such professions.

First, there is a defined field of knowledge. As previously noted, the art and science of architecture dates from the efforts of the first people who piled stone on stone to create shelter for protection from the elements. In the intervening centuries, architectural knowledge has become a well-defined and developed field of human activity.

Second, there is an accredited system of education to prepare professionals for practice. Today in the United States there are over ninety colleges and universities offering courses leading to degrees in architecture. Each of these schools is fully accredited by public and private agencies appointed to periodically review their course content and to issue accreditation credentials. These schools and the accreditation process are more fully discussed later.

Third, there is a required period of postgraduate internship followed by publicly administered examination leading to licensure to practice. Each of the fifty states plus the District of Columbia, Guam, Puerto Rico, and the Virgin Islands have laws requiring internship and examination prior to licensure to practice architecture. Internship and licensing periods in the architectural profession are more fully discussed later in the book.

Fourth, there is a recognized practicing profession dedicated to the promotion of the public interest through the advancement of its science, art, education, internship, and standards of practice. In 1857, a group of practicing architects formed The American Institute of Architects for these very purposes. Today, a majority of architects of professional status in the United States are members of the AIA and its more than 228 chapter and state associations. More than sixty other nations from Argentina to Yugoslavia have organizations similar to the AIA serving the public and the architectural professions in their own countries.

The AIA Code of Ethics

The American Institute of Architects renders dozens of services to the public and to its members on matters of architectural and urban design, education, research, office practice, building materials and services, legislation, and public relations, but its foremost function is the maintaining of the ethical and professional standards of the profession. These are embodied in its *Code of Ethics and Professional Conduct, 1987 Edition.* Excerpts from that document will illustrate the high standards of ethical and professional performance the members of AIA demand of themselves.

The *Code* is based upon the age-old realization that the profession of architecture calls for practitioners of integrity, culture, acumen, creative ability, and skill. The services of an architect may include those appropriate to the development of our physical environment, provided that the practitioner's professional integrity is maintained and that the services rendered further the ultimate goal of creating an orderly and beautiful environment. Further, it is recognized that the architect, as a professional, should seek opportunities to advance the health, safety, beauty, and well-being of the community. In other words, the architect has moral obligations to society beyond the requirements of law or business practices. In fulfilling the client's needs, the architect must always consider the public good and interest.

The *Code* also speaks to the architects' ethical and professional conduct in three ways:

1. by specifying broad principles of conduct,
2. by spelling out ethical standards that are more specific than the usual broad principles of conduct and that are both goals toward which members of the AIA should aspire and guidelines for their professional performance and behavior and,
3. by specifying rules of conduct that are mandatory, their violation being subject to disciplinary action by the AIA.

In their totality, the specifications of the *Code* lay out a rounded set of operating guidelines for the professional conduct of members in the pursuit of their professional activities wherever they may occur.

It will be sufficient for our purposes here to note examples of the various kinds of statements mentioned above, the broad principles of conduct, the more specific ethical standards, and the rules of conduct.

The five canons, or broad principles of conduct of the *Code* are as follows:

> *Canon I: General Obligations.* Members should maintain and advance their knowledge of the art and science of architecture, respect the body of architec-

tural accomplishment and contribute to its growth; learned and uncompromised professional judgement should take precedence over any other motive in the pursuit of the art and science of architecture.

Canon II: Obligations to the Public. Members should embrace the spirit and letter of the law governing their professional affairs and should thoughtfully consider the social and environmental impact of their professional activities.

Canon III: Obligations to the Client. Members should serve their clients competently and in a professional manner, and should exercise unprejudiced and unbiased judgement on their behalf.

Canon IV: Obligations to the Profession. Members should uphold the integrity and dignity of the profession.

Canon V: Obligations to Colleagues: Members should respect the rights and acknowledge the professional aspirations and contributions of their colleagues.

The Ethical Standards (abbreviated E.S.) are articulated in the *Code* with respect to each canon. For example, the Ethical Standards listed under Canon V shown above are as follows:

E.S. 5.1 Professional Environment: Members should provide their associates and employees with a suitable working environment, compensate them fairly, and facilitate their professional development.

E.S. 5.2 Professional Recognition: Members should build their professional reputation on the merits of their own service and performance and should recognize and give credit to others for the professional work they have performed.

The Rules (abbreviated by an "R" in the Code) are mandatory actions pertaining to each Ethical Standard. A rule that applies to E.S. 5.2 above is R. 5.202:

> Members leaving an employer's service shall not without the permission of the employer take designs, drawings, data, reports, notes, or other materials relating to work performed in the employer's service by members.

The force and validity of the AIA *Code of Ethics and Professional Conduct* is such that it serves as a measure of the practitioner's dedication to the architectural profession. It is not necessary to become a member of the AIA if you become registered, but similar standards of practice have frequently been cited by several states' licensing and registration agencies in their examination of candidates for licensure and enforcement of registration requirements.

THE VOCATION OF ARCHITECTURE

In broad terms, architects practice their vocation through understanding and coordinating all the resources for designing and building our physical environment. Architects in private practice render services directly to clients who compensate the architects for the time and expenses incurred in rendering the services.

In specific terms, architects can practice their vocation in the following ways:

Maintaining an office of sufficient staff, size, equipment, and financing to render professional services.

Convincing potential clients that an architect should be retained to furnish the professional services that will be required by the client's proposed projects.

Entering into a written agreement with the client for the professional services required.

Preparing a written statement, called a "program," describing in detail the requirements of the proposed project.

Executing agreements with consultants whose services may be required to supplement those of the architect.

Advising the client on the selection and suitability of sites for the proposed project.

Creating preliminary designs that satisfy the requirements of the program and the site.

Developing preliminary material selections, mechanical systems, cost analyses, construction time schedules, and financing alternatives for the proposed project.

Guiding the client to the selection of the single preliminary design that best solves the problems of program, site, cost, financing, and client wishes.

Coordinating the preparation of detailed drawings, specifications, and other contract documents required for construction of the project.

Detailing cost analyses and time schedules for the project's construction.

Assisting the client in selection of various contractors required to construct the project and assisting in the execution of contracts between the client and the selected contractors.

Administrating the construction contracts, including checking of drawings and other documents, materials and workmanship furnished by the contractor, overseeing tests required on materials, certifying payments made to the contractor, and inspecting the project at completion.

Counseling the client on maintenance, repair, and remodeling requirements after completion of the project.

Managing daily business affairs, including answering correspondence, budgeting staff workloads, hiring and directing personnel, coordinating the work of consultants, interviewing salespeople, managing investments and personnel benefits, administering insurance programs, meeting payrolls and other current obligations, billing for services, promoting new projects, entertaining present and potential clients, and directing all office activities so that they respond to the legal and ethical requirements of the practice of architecture.

Responding to professional and civic responsibilities by overseeing the internship training of professional employees and participating in the programs of local civic and professional organizations.

Nearly every project flowing through an architect's office will require most of the activities listed above. If the office has a staff of ten, chances are that it will have a minimum of six to eight major projects underway at any one time, plus several projects in the "potential" or "nearly completed" stage, and a number of smaller projects involving only partial services. The aggregate of these office and business activities, plus those imposed upon the architect by reason of civic and professional obligations, begin to give you an idea of the wide range of aptitudes required of the architect.

ATTITUDES, MOTIVATIONS, AND APTITUDES

Earlier in this chapter, we discussed the personal attitudes required of those considering a professional career and suggested that you candidly examine yourself in light of these requirements. Briefly, these attitudes were the following:

Personal character.
Capacity for human understanding.
Physical stamina and self-discipline.
Satisfaction with intrinsic rather than material rewards.

To these we can now add the aptitudes required of those considering a career in architecture. Again, you should candidly examine your own talents in light of these requirements.

Imagination. Are you a creative dreamer, an idea person? Do you usually have several suggestions on how to face up to a situation or solve a problem? Architectural practice requires the continuous production of new and creative solutions to design and construction problems.

Common sense. Do you have a faculty for sound judgment? Can you balance the ideal and desirable with the practical and achievable? Architectural solutions must be practical as well as stimulating if they are to result in construction.

Enthusiasm. Are you a person of keen and ardent interests? An architect must be able to project ideas and philosophies to others. The architect's ideas are of little value if they cannot be sold to others.

Diplomacy. Can you work with others? Can you accept their ideas and thoughts and merge them with your own? Building design and construction involves hundreds of people, all of whom look to the architect for general direction and guidance.

Visualization. Can you visualize space, color, and texture? The very essence of architecture is delight—the pleasant stimulation of the senses. The architect determines the potential delight of a space as it is designed.

Propriety. Do you have a sense of what is appropriate, timely, suitable? Successful architecture is always appropriate to its time, place, and function.

Synthesis. Can you cope with a variety of details and meld them into a coherent, rational whole? A building design incorporates tremendous amounts of detailed information.

Perseverance. Can you see a project through to its completion in spite of delays and pressures? The usual building project is stretched out over many months of work and typically encounters periods of delay while awaiting decisions and periods of overtime work to meet deadlines.

Technology. Do you have a faculty for mathematics, engineering, and other scientific and technical concerns? Contemporary building design and construction is as much a science as an art. The architect deals daily with structural, mechanical, sanitary, illuminative, power, and other technological problems.

Massing. Can you judge the distances between things, and their bulk, height, length, and width? Architecture involves size and shape, and the architect must have a good eye for the size of things.

Communication. Can you express your ideas graphically, orally, and in writing? Obviously, the architect must be able to draw—both freehand as well as mechanically, using a variety of drafting instruments and aids. These require a refined sense of color, economy of line, and the use of shade and shadow. But the practice of architecture involves an immense amount of writing also, much of it quite technical. Furthermore, there are countless occasions where the architect must rely on verbal imagery to explain ideas to others.

Management. Do you have a sense of business and personnel administration? The architect brings together many people and interests to produce a building and manages the expenditure of considerable sums of money in doing so.

If you can answer "yes" to each of these points, you have the basic aptitudes required for the rigors of a career in architecture.

TO BE AN ARCHITECT

This concludes our discussion of the responsibilities, obligations, and rewards of the professional, as well as the profession and vocation of architecture. The following chapters detail the practice of architecture and the educational, internship, and licensing requirements you must meet if you are someday to enter such practice.

By now you recognize that if you choose a career in architecture, you also choose to devote your adult life to searching out, understanding, and coordinating all the resources required for building our physical environment, and in so doing, protecting the public interest in the design and construction of buildings and the spaces between. As we have noted, the demands placed upon the professional architect are great, but so are the rewards. Architecture can be seen, felt, lived in, and used; architecture shapes our lives, adds beauty to our world, and, if fine enough, its influence will last long after its creator is gone. Most important is the fact that, if you choose to be an architect, you know that your work will make a contribution to the present and future welfare of your community.

CHAPTER 3

THE ARCHITECT'S PRACTICE

ARCHITECTS IN THE UNITED STATES TODAY

Chapter 1 reviewed examples of the wide range of career choices open to those trained in architecture. While career mobility has always been a unique feature of the American economy, contemporary cultural mores have made it even easier for people to change career orientations during their working years. This is particularly true of the white-collar worker or the professional. In the professions, one increasingly finds doctors, lawyers, engineers, and other highly trained individuals working outside of their profession, as that profession may be defined in its strictest terms. A person with several talents and motivations may be better equipped to cope with rapid changes in technology and resultant fluctuations employment opportunities. As noted throughout this book, the environmental design and construction industry has its fair share of advances and changes in the technology and economics of the industry, with the consequent ups and downs of employment opportunities. Within the industry, however, those trained and experienced in architecture have qualifications that will allow them to move into any of a number of disciplines embraced by the design professions and construction industry.

In the 1960s, 90 percent of the licensed architects in the United States were engaged in private architectural practice. Today, 84 percent are employed by private architectural or engineering firms, 3 percent by government, 3 percent by industry, 2 percent by educational institutions, and the remainder in other fields such as research or development. These figures indicate significant shifts from private architectural practice into such related design disciplines as urban planning and into other work environments—for instance, public policy agencies, development, research, writing, teaching, and industry.

In this chapter we will examine the details of private architectural practice—what it is today and what it is likely to be when you enter practice some six to eight years from now.

THE SCOPE OF ARCHITECTURAL PRACTICE

The private practice of architecture is a business in every sense of the word, and the practicing architect is a businessperson as well as a professional. The architect's primary motivation for entering practice is a professional desire to practice the art and science of architecture. However, the practitioner also expects to manage a practice profitably and ethically, thereby gaining a place in local public affairs as a successful businessperson and respected citizen. This requires constant attention to the scope of the practice—that is, to a number of general concerns affecting the content of practice and the conditions under which the profession is pursued.

Content of Practice

The first and most dominant concern is for the nature and quality of services the architect provides the client. The details of these architectural services will be discussed later in this chapter. However, note that the primary objective of the architect's services has always been, and must always remain, the union of function (the planning and relationships of spaces that meet human needs) with structure (the method of enclosing or defining space) and with beauty (that quality without which no space can qualify as architecture). This unity is what we call design; it is the very essence of architectural services.

Secondly, the architect in private practice is concerned with professional responsibilities already discussed. The prime focus is the responsibility to protect the public interest through the design of buildings and the spaces between them.

The architect's third broad area of concern is the efficient management of a practice. The architect responds to this concern for architectural design and for the services to various clients. A practice provides the architect with a base from which to render such services. The strength and viability of this base, the practice, depends upon sound business administration and management.

These three broad areas of concern for the content of practice—quality of services, professional responsibilities, and management of practice—are essentially the same for any professional in private practice—whether the practitioner's vocation is medicine, law, engineering, architecture, or another similar vocation rendering a personal service to the public. All of them are necessary to succeed. However, the conditions under which an architect practices or renders services are somewhat different from those of other professionals.

The Conditions of Practice

To begin work, the architect signs a written agreement covering the services to be rendered to the client. The doctor, lawyer, or dentist rarely, if ever, enters into a written agreement to render professional services. Written agreements between an architect and the client are necessary and desirable for a number of reasons. The process of designing and constructing a building involves large sums of money and months of work, and original intents and objectives can become confused or lost entirely unless initially set down in writing. Further, building design and construction is an incredibly complicated process, little understood by most clients. A written agreement clearly sets out for the client's benefit just what it is that is being stipulated and purchased.

Once the contract is signed, the architect depends upon a vast array of diverse talents in rendering services. Obviously, no single person is equally expert in architectural design as well as structural, mechanical, electrical, acoustical, landscape, and the dozens of other design disciplines involved in creating the typical contemporary building. Therefore, the architect depends on expert consultants in rendering services to the client. Yet, through a written agreement with the client, the architect alone is responsible to the client for the quality of the design. Consequently, the architect enters into written agreements with many consultants, covering their services to the project.

Other professionals may collaborate with related consultants to service their client. A lawyer may suggest, for instance, that a client engage an insurance consultant, or a doctor may call in a neurologist to consult on a particular problem. However, in most such situations the consultant is engaged by and is responsible to the client; there is no written agreement between the prime professional and the consultant.

In designing a building, an architect deals with tremendous sums of construction money—other people's money. The architect's services determine how these sums are allocated to the various parts of the total building project. A relatively simple error on the architect's part—a misplaced dimension, for example—can be very costly to correct. While a doctor's or lawyer's error can lead to consequences beyond correction at any price, their services do not usually encompass as many diverse details and people, nor span such a lengthy period of time as do those of the architect, and therefore, they are less exposed to chances for error that the architect.

Finally, the architect depends upon an entirely separate party—the contractor—to enable the architect to complete the various services. During the building phase, the relationship to the client changes somewhat from that in effect during the design phase of the services. During the design phase, the architect's relationship to the client is often that of seller-buyer. During the construction phase, the architect traditionally becomes the client's representative, or agent, in all dealings with the contractor.

At the same time, the architect frequently is responsible for making decisions on claims instituted by both client and contractor. In making any decisions, the architect must be an impartial judge, favoring neither client nor contractor, interested only in seeing that the building project is completed in accordance with the requirements of the drawings, specifications, and other contract documents.

A large private developer may have an in-house staff of design professionals and legal professionals. The resulting responsibilities for the independent design firm may therefore vary drastically from the norm.

An awareness and appreciation of these broad concerns for the content and conditions of private architectural practice is vital to your understanding of the scope of architectural practice. They affect each of the architect's services and office activities discussed below.

JOB DEVELOPMENT

The architect's activities in private practice begin with job development or, in plain terms, promoting services before potential clients, for there will be no opportunity for the architect to practice if there are no clients.

The client will select a particular architect for a building project in one of a number of ways. The client may already know the architect socially or through some business contact, or may be familiar with the architect's work. If this is the case, the client may simply discuss the project with the architect, following which they enter into an agreement to proceed with the required work. In other instances, the client may wish to review the qualifications and work of several architects, each of whom will discuss with the client several projects, completed or underway, that parallel the proposed project in function and size. They will each illustrate their respective qualifications to undertake the proposed work. Further, each architect may arrange for the client to visit the architect's office and one or more completed projects.

An architect may also be selected through a formal competition administered according to a detailed procedure outlined in The American Institute of Architects' Code for Competitions. This selection procedure is usually used only in connection with large or particularly significant public projects.

In any event, the demands for a constant flow of work require the architect to be in daily contact with potential clients through personal participation in civic, social, professional, and business community activities. Maintaining these contacts also has the important result of educating the public about the function of the architect in the community. Even though a particular architect may not be selected for a project, he or she will nevertheless have rendered a real service to the public and to the profession by participating in the selection process.

WRITTEN AGREEMENT

Once selected for a project, the architect and the client execute a written owner-architect agreement which specifies the services the architect will render, the amount and method of compensation to the architect, and various other contractual details. Following execution of this agreement, the architect executes parallel agreements with consultants whose special services he has determined will be required on the proposed project. The drafting of agreements is the work of lawyers, and both architect and client consult with their respective legal counsels while negotiating the agreement.

PROGRAMMING

The architect then begins planning the project. An initial step is programming all the activities which are to be housed in the building complex. The client, the architect, and the consultants all participate in developing the program. Also, contractors may be called in to advise on various construction problems uncovered during the discussion.

In brief terms, the program is a detailed description of all the functions to be included in the project and the square footage requirements for each. The program will clearly spell out relationships between the functions and any unique technical or mechanical requirements of each of the functions. It may also include preliminary cost figures, alternate structural and construction methods, materials to be considered, schedules and deadlines, and the like, which are essential to the planning.

In essence, the program will cover every item of information the architect considers essential to the efficient execution of the design services. You can appreciate that the program will vary considerably between building types—a hospital as compared to an urban renewal project, for instance—and its quality will have a real effect upon the pace and smoothness of the entire design process.

Programming the project will reveal the need for certain owner-furnished information. The architect explains the need for this information to the client, who then arranges for it to be furnished by experts in the appropriate fields, or asks the architect to arrange for its preparation. Every building project requires a site where it will be built. The client will furnish the information as to size, boundaries, topography, utilities, easements, zoning, subsurface conditions, and existing buildings.

In addition to this basic site information, other special analyses may be necessary to properly program the project.

For example, the client may be considering several types of projects or a variety of sites. Final determinations will then depend upon the findings of investigations of feasibility, market, financing, urban planning, land utilization, and zoning and site development.

Moreover, special functional requirements of the proposed project, such as auditoriums, laboratories, or computer spaces, may require that special investigations be made of humidity, waste treatment, radiation shielding, and power supply before programming can be completed. Only when all necessary information has been gathered and collated can the program be approved by both client and architect, and the actual design undertaken. Such special analyses will stretch out the programming phase of the architect's services.

DESIGN

Actual design begins with the architect's preparation of schematic designs, the simple functional or space diagrams which illustrate an analysis of the project requirements as set out in the program. In preparing schematics, the architect's intuition as an artist alternates with his or her objective judgment as an engineer or scientist. Several solutions to the design problem may be developed and presented to the client. These will be illustrated by simple line drawings showing the alternative solutions to problems of site development and volume and space interrelationships within and without the proposed structures. These will be accompanied by brief written statements generally describing the solutions regarding overall design approach, structural and mechanical systems, materials and probable costs. The architect will, of course, recommend one solution above all others, but may fully prepare alternative schematic solutions so that the client will gain the best possible understanding of the requirements of the project. A presentation is then made to the client, often employing the use of slides, simple perspectives, and models in order to secure the owner's approval of the best solution.

The approved schematic solution then enters the design development phase of the architect's services. Here it is the architect's objective to fix and illustrate the entire project in all its essentials. The materials prepared during this phase will form the basis for the construction documents and will determine the actual form and character of the final building. This phase of service is the heart of the architectural process, and full collaboration between the architect, client, and all of the special consultants is vital to the project's success.

Through this collaboration, the architect directs the preparation of drawings, outline specifications, cost statements, and other materials as may be required to bring to all the involved persons a full understanding of the intended size, shape, and cost of the proposed project. Again, at the conclusion of this phase, the architect makes any presentations necessary to fully inform the client about the details of the project. In the case of public buildings, especially where bond referendums need be held to finance projects, such as school buildings, the architect must make presentations at public hearings, zoning boards, and city or county councils. The architect will also want to participate in newspaper campaigns and other methods of public education when working on public buildings.

CONSTRUCTION DOCUMENTS

When the design development materials are approved, the architect prepares the final construction documents. These include the working drawings and specifications, which show or describe in detail all the work to be undertaken by the building contractors in the construction of the project. Their quality depends on the accuracy of cost estimates of the work and the effectiveness in constructing the building as it was designed by the architect. Thus, the architect and project consultants take special care to see that these documents are complete and accurate so that they are understandable both in the offices of the architect and the contractor and at the project site in the midst of the construction.

When the drawings are complete (often fifty or more sheets, depending on the size and complexity of the project), they are sent to the printer and the familiar blueprints are made from them. The specifications receive a final editing. Then they are printed and bound in a volume along with various bond and insurance forms, sample construction contracts, and similar contract documents prepared by the owner's legal and insurance counsel assisted by the architect. This volume will usually be hundreds of pages in length. A final, detailed cost estimate is usually made at this time to predict, as closely as possible, the actual price the contractor-bidders will quote for doing the work as designed and specified.

BIDDING OR NEGOTIATION

The printed construction documents are then distributed to various construction contractors for their bidding or negotiation. The purpose of this phase of the architect's services is to select from among qualified contractors the one that will do the work shown and described in the document for the lowest dollar figure. It usually takes contractors about thirty days to assemble their figures, whereupon they each submit their own bid to the client. The qualified contractor who submits the lowest bid is then selected by the client in consultation with the architect. An owner-contractor agreement covering the construction of the project is executed by the client and the selected contractor.

Construction may now begin. On many projects, more than nine months are consumed by the design process—that is, from the day the client selects the architect to the day the contractor moves onto the construction site. This will vary, of course, with the size and complexity of the project. Also, on some projects, particularly manufacturing facilities, construction may start almost immediately after the first schematic designs are approved. Here the client, architect, and contractor are in constant collaboration. The architect designs, the client approves, and the contractor builds on a day-by-day, hour-by-hour schedule.

CONSTRUCTION PHASE

During the construction phase, the architect provides general administration of the construction contract. The architect must check the bonds and insurance materials furnished by the contractor, check shop drawings and samples submitted by the contractor, and prepare any supplemental drawings or other interpretations required to clarify the construction documents. The architect then checks the results of specified tests, issues orders for any changes approved by the client, processes the contractor's billings to the client, checks required guarantees, and advises both client and contractor on the progress and quality of construction. A final certificate is then issued by the architect when all terms and conditions of the construction contract have been satisfactorily fulfilled.

During construction the design becomes reality. If the contractor does not properly execute the construction work, a good share of the architect's months of design work will have been wasted. Obviously the architect's management abilities are of prime importance since administering construction contracts is crucial to the fulfillment of the design.

Construction of a building can stretch from four months to over two or more years, depending upon the project's size, complexity, and weather conditions. The usual project probably takes twelve to eighteen months. Add this period to that required for design and you will note that the architect will be engaged on each project for one to two years.

POSTCOMPLETION SERVICES

When the construction of the project is complete, the client may wish to extend the original owner-architect agreement to include certain postcompletion services. These include continuing consultation on such issues as maintenance, repair, and remodeling. These services provide the client with expert counsel on how to secure the maximum usefulness of the building over its lifetime through maintenance and repair techniques which respond to the intent of the original design. Also, in rendering such services, the architect has an opportunity to study the performance of the design and to conduct on-site research in building maintenance and repair.

EXPANDING ARCHITECTURAL SERVICES

We live in a period of great change. Probably no one feels this more strongly than you as a member of the generation about to take the first step in determining your life's work. You are constantly advised of the changes that are and will be taking place in every aspect of life and are further advised to properly evaluate the impact of these changed conditions on your choice of career. This advice is vital to the present and future practice of architecture.

At one time, architectural service included only the operations to be housed in a building, the availability of land on which to construct the building, and the nature of its design and construction. The client simply told the architect that a building was needed to accommodate certain functions, that exactly so many dollars were available to spend on its design and construction, and that a certain piece of property was available on which the building was to be built. The architect provided basic architectural services within these relatively simple limits. Now these limits are changing, and the architect must modify these services to respond to this change.

Some current examples of these changing limits will illustrate the scope of the change presently taking place.

New kinds of shelters serve new functions:

The subdivision has generally replaced the individually built house.

The new town and the development complex are replacing the subdivision.

The shopping center is replacing the isolated store building.

Rehabilitation and conversion of old buildings to new uses is replacing new construction in some areas.

Automated management systems are replacing clerks and other office workers.

The use of computers and videotapes in the classroom are replacing traditional teaching methods.

Factory fabrication and prepackaging are replacing fabrication and packaging at point-of-sale.

Availability of land on which to place the building has changed.

Less and less open land is available for construction.

Relocation and demolition may frequently precede new construction.

Zoning and other land-use regulations increasingly dictate what can be built and where it can be built.

Placement of traffic and transportation facilities have a dramatic effect on the most appropriate and efficient use of land resources.

Financing and cost of constructing the building has changed.

Projects are generally larger in scope (the shopping enter *vs.* the store) and require larger sums of money.

Certain commercial interests such as the insurance industry, have tremendous sums of money available for long-term investments, such as building, while the typical client, a manufacturer for instance, wants to retain company funds for purchase of equipment and materials required in manufacturing operations. Thus institutions like insurance companies are increasingly becoming a second "client" since they will own the building upon its completion and will lease it to a tenant, such as a manufacturer.

Federal agency programs of subsidy, grants-in-aids, loans, and mortgage guaranty firms in certain construction fields may bring a third "client" into the building project.

Economic cycles of inflation/recession, and rising costs in financing, construction, and maintenance in all areas require greater ingenuity to produce cost-effective and energy-effective buildings.

These are but a few examples of the changes taking place in our time that affect the architect's services. Many more could be noted, but they all point to the fact that changing times have created conditions in which early, predesign decisions on how operations are to be housed, how land is to be assembled, and how construction is to be financed, will increasingly dictate the final architectural design. If the architect is not involved in these decisions, the project's design will be dictated by decisions that were developed previously by others.

The architectural profession is responding to these changes by expanding basic architectural services to match the requirements of our changing times. Some firms pool the resources of outside experts with their own talents to perform expanded services. Other firms frequently join in a joint venture or an association with two or more firms to provide a package of services which a single firm, acting alone, would not be able to provide. In any event, it is evident that these expanded services are becoming standard services of the architect.

Here are some of the expanded services now being offered more and more frequently by the average architectural practice.

Project Analysis Services
    Feasibility analysis
    Financial analysis
    Location and site analysis

Zoning and building code analysis
Market and merchandising analysis
Operational programming analysis
Building programming analysis

Promotional Services
Real estate and land assembly
Project development and financing
Promotional design and planning
Public relations

Design and Planning Services
Program development
Urban and regional planning
Civil engineering—traffic, transit, roads, sanitary
Landscape architecture and site development
Building design
Structural engineering
Mechanical engineering
Electrical engineering
Interior design and equipment planning
Fine arts
Architectural graphics
Special design analysis—acoustics, lighting
Cost analysis
Drawing and specifications

Construction Services
Bidding and negotiation of contracts
Administration of contracts

Job cost accounting
Construction management
Postconstruction services

Related Services
Consultation on operational programming and
building
Programming in specific building types
Research and testing
Product development and design
Consultation on building product manufacturing and
prefabrication processes

PAYMENT FOR SERVICES

The architect's fee for professional services varies as in any other profession. It depends on the architect's standing in the field, the geographic location in which the architect practices, and the kind of project to be done. However, one aspect of the architect's compensation remains the same throughout the profession: the architect's only remuneration is that received from the client. The architect does not accept commission or discounts on materials, equipment, labor costs, or any other item involved in project cost. This arrangement makes it clear that the architect's loyalty is to the client and to the project.

The amount of the architect's fee and method of payment are settled at the time the owner-architect agreement is executed. There are five principal methods of compensating the architect, although others may be agreed upon:

- A percentage of the project's construction cost
- A multiple of the architect's direct personnel expense
- A professional fee plus reimbursement of the architect's expenses
- Lump sum fee
- A salary, per diem, or hourly compensation

The percentage method is the most popular method simply because it is the most convenient to compute, is tied directly to the construction cost, and from the beginning provides the client with a firm idea of what will have to be paid for the architect's total basic services. However, the convenience of the percentage fee depends upon a clear definition of basic services.

As these services include more and more of the expanded services discussed above—most of which involve research and investigation and therefore cannot be precisely estimated in terms of time and cost—the percentage fee system is bound to fall from general usage. Many architects believe it will be replaced by a combination system where compensation for services would be computed as follows:

Programming, Schematics, and Design Development. Professional fee plus expenses, or multiple of the direct personnel expense fee.

Construction Documents. Lump sum fee.

Bidding or Negotiation. Hourly fee.

Contract Administration. Professional fee plus expenses or multiple of direct personnel expense.

Postcompletion. Hourly fee.

Other Services. Professional fee plus expenses, or multiple of direct personnel expense.

Based on general trends, a combination system of this sort will be generally employed by the profession when you enter practice some six to eight years from now.

THE ARCHITECT'S OFFICE

Every office that performs architectural services has the word "architect" written on the door. Somewhere behind that door is an individual who uses the word "architect" after his or her name and who is legally authorized to use an architect's stamp on construction documents. That is where the similarity among offices stops.

The office may contain a sole practitioner, or over two hundred people. If the office is in New England, the Pacific Northwest, or the Pacific Southwest, it is highly probable that the office will contain a sole practitioner. In the East North Central and East South Central United States, it is highly likely that the office will contain a firm of twenty or more employees. The AIA regularly publishes statistics about its membership. The 1990 edition of member statistics revealed that 22 percent of the members were sole practitioners; 58 percent of the member firms employed fewer than five people. Ninety-three percent of the firms employed fewer than twenty people. There are fewer than twenty firms in the United States with more than one hundred architect employees. These kinds of statistics also hold true in many major industrialized nations around the world.

The size of the firm often determines what kinds of work the firm can seek. Private individual clients are more likely to choose a smaller firm. The state and federal government, institutions, and large industrial clients tend to work with large firms. Firms of all sizes work with developers.

It is virtually impossible to know at the outset of an architectural career what kind of office to prepare for. As a rule of thumb, many people who begin in small offices seem to finish their careers in large firms. Those who start out in large firms, often open their own small firms in the latter years of their careers. Over half of the member firms of the AIA are under ten years old.

Most people begin a career in any design field having primarily an artistic or work satisfaction motivation. Later in their careers, economic motivation often becomes a more dominant goal, sometimes as the result of a growing family.

Every career involves the balance of these important issues. There is no question that compensation for the same level of employment is greater in a large firm. A principal in a large firm can make twice the annual salary of a sole practitioner. Even interns in a large firm earn more than small firm interns, although the difference may be only 10 or 12 percent.

It is very important to understand that the work done by employees of a small firm is quite different from that done in a very large firm. The most important difference is specialization. Generally speaking, in a small firm, everyone is expected to do more of everything. If an important job arrives in the office that requires extensive work, everyone may switch for a time to that project. One day is spent drafting, the next day may require model building, the day after could be spent on writing specifications. In a large firm, it is much more likely that the work will be more specialized. Draftspeople may never write a specification or visit a construction site. A designer may also spend a large portion of his or her career on a specific type of building. If variety becomes important, moving to another firm may become necessary.

Sole practitioners are dependent upon others for expertise they do not have. One could say that small practitioners have the largest offices, namely the rest of the community. If a bigger job comes to small office, the architect may hire a few people for a brief time or contract out the work. The essence of success for a small firm is the ability to diversify. If the market slows down in one area, they move to the next. Small offices find stability in repeat work. The more work done with the same client, the less time consumed in marketing services and customizing work methods, and the greater the profit margin. Developers with repeated projects are good clients for a small office.

Life in a large firm is more social. In many ways it is a direct extension of architectural school. Three or four people may take lunch together regularly. Work is frequently done by a team. The Christmas party is often the social highlight of the year. The whole office may go to a baseball game or a picnic in the summer.

The structure of the social environment is also demanding in a large firm. Generally speaking, working in a large firm means climbing the corporate ladder. Employees start at the bottom and work to the top. The lowest level is that of draftsperson or model maker. With experience, the draftsperson becomes a project architect responsible for a specific building design and working directly with the client or the client's representatives. With more experience the employee assumes the role of project manager, with several project architects to supervise. Above the project managers are the senior-level firm associates with overall responsibility for the work the firm performs. Finally there is the principal/partner who owns part or all of the firm and has major financial responsibility and firm leadership duties as well as the task of seeking and serving clients. Climbing this ladder in an office obviously takes both architectural experience and good social and political skills. The people at the highest levels of the firm frequently are also accomplished in the financial skills necessary to maintain a business.

The person who owns a small firm and the person who owns a large firm are probably not doing the same job each day. The sole practitioner may still be doing drafting and have major design responsibility for an admittedly small building. The person in charge of a large firm may spend most of the week in a boardroom and may never pick up a pencil. One person could be responsible for $2 million in building costs per year, the other may oversee projects worth $200 million. One person may be solving a problem about a board and a nail, the other may be meeting with the board of a corporation to resolve a master plan. These two architects may have been college classmates or taken the same Architect Registration Exam.

PRESENT AND FUTURE PRACTICE

Changing times have had their effect on the architect's services. Yet, the ultimate objectives and functions of architectural practice remain what they have always been: to design buildings and the spaces between them, and to administrate contracts for their construction. But the methods of practice are becoming very different from those traditionally employed to reach these objectives.

The American Institute of Architects, in its continuing investigation into future methods of practice, has noted nine "packages" covering management practices of the future. We will briefly review them here:

Network Planning. Master planning of project design and construction through estimating of the time required to complete each operation, its cost, and its sequence in the design and construction program. The estimates are mapped on a network plan that indicates when each service must be started and completed to make the most efficient use of time and money.

Management Science. Forecasting the probable results of managerial and administrative decisions before the decisions are made, through the use of the theory of games, probability, and statistics.

Systems Development. Solving design problems through research into space relationships, human performance under varying environmental conditions, and similar psychological factors.

Construction Cost Management. Evaluating and managing the cost of construction through precise measurements and control of the quantity and quality of materials and labor throughout the construction of the project.

Design Quality Control. Measuring and evaluating the quality and reliability of design through the analysis and feedback of design performance.

Communications. Improving communications between persons involved in the design and construction processes through new systems of receiving, recording, indexing, retrieving, and using information.

Reproduction Systems Technology. Improving duplication of graphic and written materials through use of new photographic and videotaping devices for handling and displaying construction documents.

Computer Technology. Automation and computerization of standardized and time-consuming design and management operations.

Automated Graphical Systems. Increasing the flexibility and breadth of the design process through use of electronic plotting and display units which automatically call up and incorporate previously stored information into design studies.

Architectural office practice procedures have been changing slowly. These nine "packages" of techniques now emerging within the profession are an indication of the immense changes that will take place in the next twenty to thirty years.

YOUR PRACTICE

This concludes our discussion of the details of architectural practice as we know it today. The next chapter discusses the education and licensing requirements you must meet before you can enter the community as an architect.

Chances are that when you enter your own practice, you will be a person with quite different qualifications from those of the present-day architect, for the expanded services and new techniques of practice discussed in this chapter will radically affect architectural education and practice in your time. These changes are bound to multiply at an ever-increasing rate. Such is the nature of the automated society in which we live.

These changes, as important as they will be to your practice as an architect and to your responsibility for continuing self-education as a professional, will not alter the basic architectural mission, the creation of humanity's physical environment. Rather, the changes will broaden your practice by freeing you of much of the hand-work now associated with research, analysis, and computation, affording greater control over management and design processes, and permitting you to spend more time on creative design.

CHAPTER 4

EDUCATION FOR ARCHITECTURE

Your elementary and secondary education form the foundation for your education toward a professional career. They had much to do with your decision to consider a selected number of possible career options amongst the thousands available in today's economy. You are now ready to select a formal course of instruction that will prepare you for your occupation. It is an extremely important consideration, for your commitment to your education will be extraordinary—in terms of both financial investment and intellectual dedication.

You have begun your selection early in your schooling by choosing certain courses in junior and senior high school. Thereafter you will invest five to eight years of your life and anywhere from $5,000 to $25,000 per year for your college education.

Because of these considerable investments, it makes good sense that, prior to making your career choice, you have a firm insight into the challenges and opportunities offered by a career in architecture, that you make a candid appraisal of your attitudes and abilities, and that you gain a broad understanding of the educational and licensing requirements you must satisfy to enter the profession.

This chapter discusses these educational and licensing requirements and the tuition and other costs associated with them. Before we proceed, however, we should briefly review careers in architecture and the attitudes required of those who choose to enter the profession and vocation of architecture.

THE CONSTRUCTION INDUSTRY

As an architect, your work will be combined with that of many other disciplines in the construction industry—urban planning, engineering, education, contracting and financing, to name a few. Your contribution to the process of creating buildings will be one of leadership, and your decisions will put these other disciplines into action.

In pursuit of your career, you may find that one or more of these other disciplines is as attractive to you as architecture. If so, you will further find that your basic education and training in architecture have prepared you to move with competence into these other disciplines with a relatively small amount of additional training.

The employment prospects for those trained in architecture are good. Construction is cyclical—that is, it rises and falls with the general economy. However, since it is such an important part of the nation's economy, federal and local governments have developed public project policies designed to minimize economic fluctuations. Public expenditures for construction projects are encouraged in times of depression and scaled down or withheld in times of inflation in an effort to stabilize the flow of investment.

The work of the architect is also cyclical, partly because of the nature of construction, but is determined more by the nature of the client or buying public. A client may speculate for some time on whether to build, but once having decided, is anxious to see the project completed. Therefore, for most projects, the architect is obliged to be patient while the client is making a decision and then to bring all available resources to bear on completing the project as soon as possible following the client's favorable decision. Deadlines, overtime, and evening work are commonplace for the architect.

THE PROFESSION OF ARCHITECTURE

The architect is a professional and, as such, holds a primary concern for people—for their health, their safety, and their general welfare. The architect reveals this concern by exercising judgment in solving the client's building problems. These decisions are as often based on moral and technical issues as on the monetary issues involved. This philosophy of service to others before self demands a dedication to certain ideals easily overlooked in the pressures of today's materialistic society. The opportunity for intrinsic rewards is immense: the satisfaction of exercising independent judgment, the joy of creation, the appreciation of those served, the recognition by others of your professional achievements.

Persons trained in architecture need not confine their talents to design. A career in architecture offers opportunities in sales, technical writing, contract law, administration, business and personnel management, cost accounting, computer science, and many other disciplines in addition to design. Within the practice of architecture, there are as many career opportunities as can be found in almost any other discipline. It merely remains for you to determine which turn you wish your career to take. This determinations rests primarily upon your own attitudes, motivations, and aptitudes.

REVIEW OF ATTITUDES, MOTIVATIONS, AND APTITUDES

Now that you are aware of the challenges, opportunities, and rewards of architecture, perhaps you should review the list of character traits needed to become an architect (see chapter 2). How do your personal characteristics measure up to the requirements of the profession?

Personal Character. Can you meet the demands placed on those who act as professional advisers?

Human Understanding. Can you work with all kinds of people?

Stamina and Discipline. Do you have the self-discipline for years of formal education and a lifetime in self-education?

Rewards. If necessary, will you accept intrinsic rewards in lieu of material rewards?

Imagination. Do you generate creative ideas?

Common Sense. Do you have sound judgment?

Enthusiasm. Do you have keen and ardent interests?

Diplomacy. Can you meld your ideas and interests with those of others?

Visualization. Can you visualize space, color, texture?

Propriety. Do you have a sense for what is appropriate to the time and place?

Synthesis. Can you cope with a variety of details?

Perseverance. Can you stick with a project in spite of delays and other pressures?

Technology. Do you have a faculty for mathematics, engineering, and other scientific or technical matters?

Dimensions. Can you judge distances, proportions, and visual relationships?

Communications. Can you draw, write, and speak well enough to effectively communicate your ideas to others?

Management. Do you have a sense of business and personnel administration?

As improbable as it may seem, the truly successful professional architect exhibits all these characteristics. To be sure, some were developed following formal education, but the aptitudes were there all the time waiting to be revealed by the demands of a professional career. The earlier they are revealed, the earlier you will know the satisfaction of matching your attitudes, motivations, and aptitudes to the challenges and opportunities of a career in architecture.

PREPARATION WHILE IN HIGH SCHOOL

The education and experience required for a career in architecture is acquired in stages. The process begins with your choice of an architectural career and proceeds through your formal schooling, internship, licensure, and professional years. Once started the process never really stops.

Formal schooling and internship, from secondary school to licensure, will usually consume from eight to ten years. This allows for five to seven years of professional study and three to four years of internship. While this process cannot be appreciably accelerated, even for the gifted student, it can be made more meaningful and productive by an early career decision. If you make your career decision early in your secondary school years, you will tend to focus your attention on those junior and senior high school courses and activities that stimulate the talents and interests vital to a successful architect.

As you approach your decision on an architectural career, consult your school's vocational guidance counselor. The counselor will assist you in making this early decision by helping you identify your talents and motivations, matching these against the requirements of the profession, and suggesting secondary school courses and extracurricular activities that will strengthen your overall capabilities. Later in your secondary education, the counselor will focus your attention on those colleges and universities that offer courses in architectural education that most nearly match your particular interests and capabilities.

Among the most important skills required in architectural education and practice are an ability for communications and a power for scientific reasoning. Consequently, artistic, linguistic, mathematic, and scientific skills are important prerequisites to a college architectural curriculum. Your aptitude in these areas should be identified and developed as early as possible.

Specific entrance requirements vary from college to college. Certain guidelines may be mentioned, but you must always check the requirements of the particular school of your choice. General guidelines include graduation from an accredited high school, with rank in the upper one-third or one-fourth of the graduating class; or, in some cases, with a "B" average; 15 or 16 units total in:

English, 3–4 units
Mathematics, 3–4 units
Science, 2–3 units
Social Studies, 1–2 units
Foreign Language, 1–2 units
Other, 1–2 units (history, economics, other appropriate electives)

Beyond your secondary school academic record, certain other materials may have to be submitted, including:

Record of Scholastic Aptitude Test and other specialized tests of the College Entrance Examination Board (CEEB) administered by the Educational Testing Service, Box 592, Princeton, New Jersey 08540, or Box 1025, Berkeley, California, 94704. Some schools also will accept test scores from the American College Testing Program (ACT), Box 168, Iowa City, Iowa, 52243.

Recommendation of school principal and other qualified persons

Health record

Evidence of personal qualities, educational and career objectives, basic skills in visual arts

Record of any special tests administered by the particular school to which you are applying

These add up to a most impressive set of academic and extracurricular requirements. They emphasize the value of an early decision on a career and an early investigation of the precise requirements of the particular school you choose. Again, you should discuss these matters with your school's vocational counselor early in your secondary schooling. The counselor will have many suggestions on how you should shape your secondary school activities to prepare for college admission. Although it is the rare eighth-grader who is actively preparing for his or her career at such an early age, the decision process might be started then.

Whenever you begin, the first step is to consider two or three careers, including architecture, that interest you. Then you need to research which colleges offer the best training in these fields. If possible, you should match your academic and extracurricular choices to the admissions requirements at those schools. Closer to the date of your graduation, you will need to narrow your choices of schools and begin visiting college campuses in person to select the one that will best meet your needs.

In implementing your educational plan, you must remember two principal points. First, you must make your own arrangements to contact colleges, take the required tests, and write for information. Your guidance counselor can advise you on these matters, but it is up to you to carry them out. Second, most arrangements must be made months in advance. For instance, many college admissions applications must be submitted in February for September matriculation.

Do not be overly concerned if your preparation thus far has not followed a specific route intended to result in a career in architecture. Many people do not establish their career goals until much later in college or even after graduation. For any important voyage, however, once you know where you want to go, it always helps to have a map. Once you commit your life to being an architect, you can say you are one. However, it takes some very specific steps to convince the rest of the world to allow you to practice your profession.

To skip college is not in your best interest professionally or financially. Likewise, merely entering any available college is a luxury you cannot afford. When you enter a course of instruction, it should be with the full expectation that you can meet its required level of performance as well as manage its costs. Therefore, choosing the college program that is best suited to you is extremely important. This may mean that you should start in a junior college or small liberal arts college, later moving on to a larger university for your professional work. Or, you may find that your first years are best spent in a college in your home town where you can live at home, saving up for the last years at a more distant school. In any event, the choice is not just a school or combination of schools, but a total undergraduate and professional educational program that will meet your particular needs.

In searching for the academic program that is best for you, there are three groups of factors you should consider. The first focuses on you:

How good a student are you? If you are in the top ten percent of the class, your choice of colleges is largely unlimited. Below this, your choice is somewhat restricted. This is to your benefit, for if you entered a school having higher performance requirements than you can match, you might soon be buried under an impossible academic load.

What kind of school is best for you? Are you prepared to go immediately into a college curriculum that leads directly to a professional degree in architecture, or should you spend the first years in a liberal arts college?

What size school is best for you? The relative advantages and disadvantages of large and small schools are obvious, but too often are not adequately considered by many young people.

In debating these questions, you have three excellent resources at hand: your parents and/or other adult family members and friends, your school's vocational guidance counselor, and any of your friends currently in their final undergraduate or early graduate years. Your friends who are currently completing their college work have the freshest possible view on what it is like to attend today's college or university.

The second group of factors to consider in choosing a school focuses on the college:

Are the school's architectural programs accredited by the National Architectural Accrediting Board? If its programs are not accredited, the school's graduates may receive only partial credit toward those academic requirements needed to apply for licensing examinations in certain states. The types of programs offered by schools accredited by NAAB are not necessarily identical. In fact, they may vary considerably from school to school. As you plan your visits to various schools, you will want to brief yourself ahead to time on the program choices. Such information can be gained by writing each school separately or by securing a copy of the publication *Guide to Architecture Schools in North America.* The publication can be ordered from the Association of Collegiate Schools of Architecture, 1735 New York Avenue, N.W., Washington, D.C. 20006. This is a very complete collection of information that will brief you on almost every question you may want to ask when you visit schools.

What are the specific admission and degree requirements of the school, and what does the school have to offer? What requirements must you meet to earn your degree in architecture? What is the content of the required and elective courses? What level degree will you earn? How many years will it take? How large is the college student body? What are the qualifications of its faculty? What kind of physical facilities are available both for academic work and for residence? These facts are related in the catalog of each college. Also, they are briefed in the statistical information publication available from the Association of Collegiate Schools of Architecture at the address noted above.

Your best source of guidance in discussing any college is the college itself. If possible you should plan to visit the schools of your choice and talk directly with their admissions officers and with the faculty members responsible for interviewing possible applicants. Recent graduates are also good resource persons. Older alumni can be helpful even though most colleges have changed considerably in the last decade. Of course, your guidance counselor is usually your first source of information and your best overall adviser in comparing facts gathered from a group of schools in which you may be interested.

The third group of factors to consider focuses on costs:

What does the school cost, and how will you pay for tuition? What are the tuition costs and other fees for resident students? For nonresident students? What is covered by tuition payments? By fees? When are they payable? What are the estimates of the cost of room and board? Are there scholarships available? Jobs on campus? Is this a work-study program school?

Have you considered travel costs to and from home and college? Will you need to finance your education through loans such as personal, college, private organization, or government loan?

Actual dollar costs for tuition, fees, room, board, travel, and incidental expenses vary considerably throughout the over one hundred architectural schools in the United States and Canada. However, we can offer some guidelines.

State-supported school in your own state. Budget at least $5,000 to $8,000 per year plus travel.

State-supported school outside your own state. Budget at least $7,000 to $10,000 per year plus travel.

Private school. Budget at least $9,000 to $25,000 per year plus travel.

After bringing together all the costs associated with each school you are considering, you should make out a tentative budget covering the full college period and detail as accurately as possible the first two years. Only then will you appreciate the considerable investment you are about to make in your education. Colleges often assist students in outlining a complete financing program. Also, your parents and your school's vocational guidance counselor will be of vital assistance here.

COLLEGE COURSEWORK

Earlier in this chapter we gave certain guidelines on college admission requirements. Here we present general guidelines on the curriculum offered in the typical school of architecture. Again, we emphasize that these are general guidelines only and that you must always check the course content of the particular school of your choice.

First Year

    History of visual arts
    Basic design and composition
    Differential and integral calculus, analytic geometry
    Basic physical sciences

Basic economics
Sociology of American Society
Literature and interpretation
European history

Second Year
Architectural drawing, architectural composition
Ancient and medieval architecture
Basic computers
Basic structures
English literature
American government
Introductory philosophy, religion

Third Year
Site planning
Basic computers
Architectural design, analysis of architectural
     composition
Materials of construction
Renaissance and modern architecture
Drawing, color
Structural engineering
American art and civilization

Fourth Year
Architectural design, analysis of architectural
     composition
Methods of construction
Advanced structural engineering

Urban sociology
Specialized courses in art

Fifth Year
Architectural design synthesis
Illumination, mechanical equipment
Structural planning
Community planning

Sixth Year
Architectural composition
Illumination, environmental engineering
Professional practice, architectural research
Dynamics of structures
Advanced studies in history and development of art and
architecture
Thesis—individual research and analysis on a subject
of particular interest to you

As mentioned previously, programs vary from school to school. Thus, some schools offer these subjects in four-year courses leading to a Bachelor of Fine Arts degree (BFA), with two additional years to earn a Master of Fine Arts (MFA) in architecture degree. Other schools offer a five-year course leading to a Bachelor of Architecture (BA). A few schools offer a Bachelor of Science (BS) in architecture degree earned after six years of formal courses alternating with cooperative periods of work in the professional field. In all events, check each college's course information closely to be sure that you understand its content and length and know whether or not the school is fully accredited by the NAAB.

College admissions is a big business. Each year one to two million high school graduates apply for admission to our nation's colleges and universities. Some schools receive thousands of applications and can eventually enroll less than 10 percent of those who apply. You can get a head start on this process, and avoid many of the tensions associated with it, if you follow the suggestions we have discussed here while you are in secondary school and choosing your college architectural program. It is up to you to start the process and to keep it moving once it is underway.

COLLEGE DAYS

Many of your experiences as a student in an architectural curriculum will be similar to those of college students in other curricula. However, there are a few unique experiences in an architectural program, and you will be interested to know of them and what they entail.

For instance, the laboratory course is common to the architectural curriculum. The architectural student's principal laboratory is the drafting room and the art studio for courses in composition and design, drawing and sketching, drafting and presentation, and painting and sculpture. All of these activities involve a great deal of experimentation in the materials and techniques of the visual arts and consume great chunks of a student's time. Because of the equipment involved—drafting boards, T-squares, computers, and a sizable quantity of paper, paints, and other material—almost all of this lab work is done at school. In most schools, the labs are open all night as the students in architecture push to meet a morning deadline.

Since much of the student's work is done in visual media, there is a great deal of brainstorming, kibitzing, and criticism of each other's work. Free advice is always in great supply at any art or architectural school. Consequently, open competition along with a full exchange of ideas is characteristic of architectural schools. Out of this grows a great camaraderie among the students. Traditionally, confrontations, discussions, debates, and occasionally comic relief through a healthy amount of practical joking are hallmarks of the architectural school.

The talents of the architectural students lend themselves admirably to the creation, design, and preparation of graphics, stagecraft, layouts for school publications, decorations, and constructions for various campus happenings. The architectural student never wants for involvement in extracurricular activities. The biggest problem may well be avoiding over-involvement, for the architectural curriculum is normally so demanding that very little time remains to devote to nonacademic pursuits.

The student of architecture should have no problem finding summer employment that will offer personal and career development. The most valuable summer employment puts the student in direct contact with the building process— clerking in a building supply outlet or even a general hardware store, working as a rodman on a surveying team, working for a general or mechanical contractor, serving as an office helper/assistant in an architect's or engineer's office, or working for any of the thousands of retail, whole-sale, or manufacturing businesses that serve the building industry, including blueprint shops, brick and masonry yards, and lumber mills.

Architecture is tangible. It is best understood when seen, felt, and experienced firsthand. Therefore, travel is an essential part of an architect's education. Personal finances may not allow a trip around the United States, Canada, Mexico or other countries until well after your graduation, but you should plan to travel as much as possible and as early in your career as finances will permit. While in school, you will take field trips under school sponsorship; you may even be fortunate enough to be awarded a scholar-ship just for travel. In the meantime, you have your own home town, the city in which the college is located, and all the points in between. Moreover, every region in the United States has something to be seen which will be of value to your architectural education. Make these your travel objec-tives for the moment.

It is characteristic of the architect to be minutely obser-vant of all surroundings, and you should begin now to train yourself to really see everything you look at—both natural and constructed objects—analyzing each for its function, its materials, its structure, and its relationship to other things.

During your third year of college, you will need to give serious attention to the possibility of going to graduate school. Historically, the architect has completed the re-quired formal education with a bachelor's degree, but this has changed. The qualified student is encouraged to consider very seriously courses to earn a master's degree in architecture, structural engineering or urban planning. Another possibility might be earning a second bachelor's degree in a field related to architecture and construction, such as landscape architecture; civil, electrical, or mechanical engineering; law; economics; or business administration. As has been repeatedly pointed out in this book, the architect's field of interest is broadening to include every activity that affects our physical environment. This broadening interest requires leadership from those trained in multiple disciplines. If you have the basic qualifications for this leadership, it would be wise for you to train for this role by earning a graduate degree.

YOUR TRAINING AS AN INTERN

Employment after graduation means a great deal more than an opportunity to earn a living. Your first job after graduation is also your first step in fulfilling the period of internship required by your state registration board. Usually three years of internship after graduation are required, although this can vary because of military service, summer employment, and so forth. The purpose of internship is, of course, to learn how the theories, knowledge, and skills acquired in architectural school find their use and application in architects' services to the public. Therefore, you must serve your apprenticeship under the direction and control of an architect registered to practice in the state in which you plan to apply for registration. You will receive a full and regular salary during this period from the architect who employs you. You are not obligated to stay in the same office for all three years of your internship.

In looking for that first job, you should consider firms of good reputation where you will be exposed to all phases of practice. This may mean a small-to-medium-size office or a larger firm for experience in projects involving large numbers of design, construction, and business management specialists. Your school's job placement office will assist you in contacting architects interested in current graduates, or you can simply write to firms of your own interest and knowledge, stating clearly and concisely your qualifications as you see them and the salary range you consider equitable. The architect will respond, suggesting an interview if your application fits the job description. Be punctual for your interview, and be prepared to illustrate the attitudes, aptitudes, and motivations previously discussed in this chapter.

A portfolio presenting your training and any experience you have accumulated will interest the architect. The architect's principal interest will focus on your participation in the discussion because it reveals your attitudes and motivations.

While serving your internship, you will learn primarily through observation and self-study and will gain experience from explanations and criticisms of your work. In most offices, there is no formal procedure or schedule for your internship work. Consequently, it is primarily your own responsibility to seek a wide range of job experiences. You should avoid excessive specialization by seeking experience in the whole range of tasks performed in your employer's practice.

In recent years the National Council of Architectural Registration Boards and the American Institute of Architects have been developing and refining and Intern Development Program (IDP). IDP's purpose is to provide to interns (and their employers) a structured program assuring each intern of a wide range of practical work tasks in preparation for state examination and registration. IDP is available in all jurisdictions in the United States and will ultimately be offered by all architectural offices. In considering your first employment opportunity, you should inquire as to the availability of IDP in each interview situation. Results of IDP to date demonstrate quite clearly that the program benefits each intern fortunate enough to have participated in the program.

When first employed, your duties will likely be that of simple drafting and lettering jobs to help complete presentation and working drawings. As your skill develops, you will be given responsibility to fully prepare working drawings for certain details or for selected portions of the project. Later, your work will include structural computations and specifications writing.

With this experience in hand, you will be assigned increasing responsibility to prepare initial designs and help oversee the production of contract documents for an entire project. This will mean working with the client to determine the building's design costs, and the direction of other employees in the architect's office.

This comprehensive experience is not easily obtained in three short years of internship. You and your employer will need to work together to be sure you are exposed to the maximum range of office and project experiences. To assure that you are benefiting from this maximum exposure, it is recommended that you maintain a training record during your internship. As you approach graduation, initial materials on your career development should be assembled. As you accumulate further materials, they will serve as a report to your state registration board at the time of your examination for registration and will also illustrate your competence for practice to employers and future clients. The report will include the following items.

A general information form with resumes of your education and training.

Sketches, presentation drawings, and photographs of models representing your own work in design.

Copies of prints of working drawings you have prepared.

Copies of prints of structural, mechanical, electrical, and architectural details to indicate your competence in the coordination of construction.

Copies of programming studies, cost analyses, specification sheets, and other reports you have prepared to illustrate your competence in preparation of technical materials.

Photographs of the construction of buildings for which you have administered the construction contract. Referencing these photographs to the drawings, details, specifications, and other materials cited above is desirable.

Letters from employers giving duration and type of work you performed for them and certifying that examples of work shown represent your work.

List of honors and awards, special study, travel, teaching experiences, publications or any other related activities to emphasize your breadth of interests, experience, and accomplishments.

The report will demonstrate whether your preparation for practice is adequate. The board may deny the privilege of further examination if the report indicates that your knowledge and training for practice is inadequate.

EXAMINATION AND REGISTRATION

Each of the fifty states, Guam, the Virgin Islands, the Northern Mariana Islands, Puerto Rico, and the District of Columbia have laws regulating the practice of architecture. There is some variation among these laws, but generally, they prohibit the use of the title "architect" for those who are not licensed and make it unlawful to practice architecture without a license. It is imperative that you be familiar with the details of the legal requirements in your state. Three references are of value here: *IDP Guidelines: Graduating into Architecture,* available from your own state board; the *Circular of Information No. 1,* available from the National Council of Architectural Registration Boards (NCARB); and *Architect's Handbook for Professional Practice,* available from the American Institute of Architects (AIA). You should secure these reference materials early in your schooling, preferably during your secondary school preparations, so that you fully understand the licensing requirements upon which all of your education focuses. After all, your licensing as an architect is the major objective of all your schooling.

The Architect Registration Examination (ARE) is administered by the state board twice a year in one or more cities in a state and takes four days to complete. Reference material is provided for some portions of the examinations, and each portion will typically take from three to twelve hours to complete. Refresher courses are offered in many cities, and information may be secured by contacting your local AIA chapter office.

Those who fail the state board examination may retake those portions failed, in conformance with the reexamination provisions of the particular state board involved. Once you have secured a license to practice in a particular state, it is possible to become registered in other states through a process of reciprocity, or by obtaining an NCARB certificate, which is a requirement for reciprocity in many states. This system eliminates the need for further examinations. In all events, you should become familiar with the examination and registration requirements in the state where you wish to practice.

The Architect Registration Exam

The Architect Registration Examination as administered by the National Council of Architectural Registration Boards (NCARB) has the following four-day schedule:

DAY ONE

Construction Documents and Services
(3 hours, 135 questions)
Materials and Methods
(2 1/2 hours, 135 questions)
Mechanical, Plumbing, and Electrical Systems
(2 1/2 hours, 135 questions)

DAY TWO

Structural Technology—General and Long Span
(3 1/2 hours, 135 questions)
Structural Technology—Lateral Forces
(1 3/4 hours, 70 questions)
Site Design—Written
(1 3/4 hours, 85 questions)

DAY THREE

Pre-design
(3 1/2 hours, 160 questions)
Site Design—Graphic
(2 3/4 hours, 6 graphic vignettes)

DAY FOUR

Building Design
(12 hours, 1 graphic problem)

PROFESSIONAL PRACTICE AND CONTINUING EDUCATION

Once you have earned your license to practice architecture, you may choose to work toward a partnership in an established firm, or to establish your own firm by yourself or in partnership with one or more colleagues. You may choose to teach or do research for a large institution, or go into urban planning, building product sales and manufacturing, or one of many other salaried positions in public or private employ. The possibilities are almost unrestricted, and the direction you choose will probably become clear during your internship.

However, one important consideration underlies all these possibilities: do not put off earning your license to practice architecture! It is essential to your career.

Too many young people let the opportunity to become registered slip away from them after graduation by going directly into teaching, urban planning, or some other field that does not afford them the opportunity to fulfill the requirements of internship—that is, three to four years in the practice of architecture under the control and direction of a licensed architect. Consequently, they are never eligible to take the state board examination. Later, they find that in their years away from school and practice, they have forgotten much of the technical knowledge required to pass the examination and that refresher courses just aren't sufficient to prepare them for some portions of it. Without the license, they are denied full accreditation as an architect, and their career potential is compromised. Increasingly, the first measure of each one of us is based upon the degrees and licenses we hold, and it makes supreme good sense to be sure you receive every credential you have earned.

Continuing progress in the techniques of environmental design and construction will present new challenges to you every day of your career, challenges to expand your knowledge, skills, and competence, and to guide younger associates along the path you already know so well. The AIA and other industry associations offer a multitude of professional development opportunities through conventions, symposia, research, publications, and participation in the work of local and national association committees.

The architectural and other environmental design professions conduct extensive studies in education for the technician in junior college, for the student in professional school and for the licensed architect and others already engaged in professional practice. You will benefit from these studies during your years of schooling and internship, and, eventually, you will also have partial responsibility for their further advancement.

These challenges are considerable and will be constantly demanding of your time and energies. But, as we have said before, you will be a professional to whom society looks as a guardian of its health, its safety, and its general welfare. For those who would answer these challenges, the demands could not be less.

CHAPTER 5

ARCHITECTURAL RESOURCES

This chapter explains sources important to your further understanding of what architecture is all about, what an architect does, the training and experience required for licensing to practice, and which schools offer accredited courses in architecture.

The architects in your own home town are an excellent source of career information. You should not hesitate to telephone the local chapter of The American Institute of Architects and ask for the names and addresses of one or more practitioners whom you might call upon to discuss your choice of career. If your home town does not have a local AIA chapter office, simply select the name of a practitioner from the yellow pages of the telephone directory, call and explain your mission, and ask for an appointment for an office interview. Be on time, have your questions firmly in mind, and record important points for later reference. You will find the experience immensely rewarding, and the practitioner will be pleased to have had an opportunity to assist you in the choice of a career.

In preparing for such an interview, you should review the questions you expect to ask with your vocational counselor. Chances are that you have already talked with the counselor about your search for a vocation and found the discussion to be of help in thinking out solutions to the many questions that have come to mind. By discussing your interview with the counselor before and after your visit to the architect's office, you will get the maximum benefit from your interview.

If by chance you haven't yet called upon your school's vocational counselor, or would like to know more about career planning before you do have your meeting, it is recommended that you check references in your school's library under "Vocational Guidance." There should be several available which will provide you with a general background on choosing a vocation.

BOOKS

There are thousands of books available on the subject of architecture. Many of them go into great detail on special subjects within the general field, such as the history of architecture, various aspects of office practice, or famous modern architects. Here we list several references which, if taken together, will give you a comprehensive overview of the art, science, and practice of architecture.

Write to Architects and Planners Book Service, Macmillan Books Clubs, Inc., Front and Brown Streets, Riverside, New Jersey 08370, requesting a listing of the books they are currently offering. In any one month this service makes available some 25 to 35 books on all aspects of environmental design. Reviewing these listings will introduce you to the wide variety of opportunities available to those trained in the field of environmental design.

Here are some other suggestions.

Architecture. The World Book Encyclopedia, Volume 1, World Book, Incorporated, 1992. Chicago. A well-written, profusely illustrated, and concise treatment of the field.

Space, Time and Architecture. Sigfried Giedien, The Harvard University Press, Cambridge, Massachusetts, 2nd Edition, 1963. A classic study giving countless insights into the moving processes of life and enabling the layperson to assess the architect's contributions to social history and urban development.

The Architect's Handbook of Professional Practice. The American Institute of Architects, Washington, D.C., 1988 and subsequent editions. A comprehensive summation of business and management procedures, and contract documents employed in contemporary architectural practice. This reference may not be available in your local library, but any architect will have it in the office, or you can review it in the library at any school of architecture.

Professional Options. Chapter 1.4, *The Architect's Handbook of Professional Practice,* The American Institute of Architects, Washington, D.C., 1988. Information for this chapter was in large part developed by Stephen Kliment, FAIA. It is available as a publication separate from the rest of the *AIA Handbook.* Single copies may be ordered at no cost. It highlights the changes taking place in the practice of architecture, the new techniques and procedures required of traditional practice, and the newest and emerging career options available to architects. The material provides insights into how architecture will be practiced by the time you enter the field. A copy can be purchased from the AIA Bookstore, 1735 New York Avenue, N.W., Washington, D.C. 20006.

GENERAL EDUCATION INFORMATION

A most convenient general reference for all information relating to architectural education is the Director, Education Programs, The American Institute of Architects, 1735 New York Avenue, N.W., Washington, D.C. 20006. That office can give you general information on any aspect of architectural education, financial aid, internship and licensing, and career and professional concerns. Further, they can direct you to other organizations providing detailed information on these concerns.

SCHOOLS OF ARCHITECTURE

The list of schools of architecture with programs accredited by the National Architectural Accrediting Board, Inc., is issued by the NAAB, 1735 New York Avenue, N.W., Washington, D.C. 20006. It lists all schools of architecture in the United States that offer programs leading to a professional degree acceptable to the profession and the law. NAAB also publishes a list of Canadian Schools of Architecture recognized by the Royal Architectural Institute of Canada. These lists are revised annually and are valid in detail only until the next lists are issued. Copies may be secured, free of charge, by writing the NAAB at the address above.

Schools within the United States include the institutions listed below. Not all of them offer accredited undergraduate degree programs. Some are exclusively graduate schools.

Andrews University
  Department of Architecture
  Berrien Springs, Michigan 49104

Arizona, University of
  College of Architecture
  Tucson, Arizona 85721

Arizona State University
  College of Architecture & Environmental Design
  Tempe, Arizona 85287-1605

Arkansas, University of
  School of Architecture
  Fayetteville, Arkansas 72701

Auburn University
  School of Architecture
  Auburn, Alabama 36849-5313

Ball State University
  College of Architecture and Planning
  Muncie, Indiana 47306

Boston Architectural Center
  320 Newbury Street
  Boston, Massachusetts 02115

California, University of
  Department of Architecture
  College of Environmental Design
  Berkeley, California 94720

California, University of
  Graduate School of Architecture and Urban Planning
  Los Angeles, California 90024-1467

California Polytechnic State University, Architecture Dept.
  School of Architecture and Environmental Design
  San Luis Obispo, California 93407

California State Polytechnic University
  College of Environmental Design
  Department of Architecture
  Pomona, California 91768

Carnegie-Mellon University
  College of Fine Arts
  Department of Architecture
  Pittsburgh, Pennsylvania 15213

Catholic University of America
  Department of Architecture & Planning
  Washington, D.C. 20064

Cincinnati, University of
  Department of Architecture and Interior Design
  College of Design, Architecture, Art and Planning
  Cincinnati, Ohio 45221-0016

The City College of the City
  University of N.Y.
  School of Architecture and Environmental Studies
  New York, New York 10031

Clemson University
  College of Architecture
  Clemson, South Carolina 29634

Colorado, University of
  School of Architecture and Planning
  Denver, Colorado 80217-3364

Columbia University
  Graduate School of Architecture, Planning and Preservation
  New York, New York 10027

Cooper Union
  The Irwin S. Chanin School of Architecture
  New York, New York 10003

Cornell University
  Department of Architecture
  College of Architecture, Art and Planning
  Ithaca, New York 14853-6701

Detroit, University of
  School of Architecture
  Detroit, Michigan 48221

Drexel University
  Department of Architecture
  Nesbitt College of Design
  Philadelphia, Pennsylvania 19104

Drury College
  Hammons School of Architecture
  Springfield, Missouri 65802

Florida A & M University
  School of Architecture
  Tallahassee, Florida 32307

Florida, University of
  College of Architecture
  Gainesville, Florida 32611

Georgia Institute of Technology
  College of Architecture
  Atlanta, Georgia 30332-0155

Hampton Institute
  School of Pure and Applied Science
  Department of Architecture
  Hampton, Virginia 23668

Harvard University
  Graduate School of Design
  Cambridge, Massachusetts 02138

Hawaii, University of
  Department of Architecture
  Honolulu, Hawaii 96822

Houston, University of
  College of Architecture
  Houston, Texas 77204-4431

Howard University
  School of Architecture & Planning
  Washington, D.C. 20059

Idaho, University of
  Department of Architecture
  College of Art & Architecture
  Moscow, Idaho 83843

Illinois Institute of Technology
  College of Architecture
  Chicago, Illinois 60616

Illinois at Chicago, University of
   School of Architecture
   Chicago, Illinois 60680

Illinois, University of
   School of Architecture
   608 East Larado Taft Drive
   Champaign, Illinois 61820

Iowa State University
   Department of Architecture
   Ames, Iowa 50011-3093

Kansas State University
   Department of Architecture
   College of Architecture and Design
   Manhattan, Kansas 66506

Kansas, University of
   School of Architecture and Urban Design
   Lawrence, Kansas 66045-2249

Kent State University
   School of Architecture and Environmental Design
   Kent, Ohio 44242

Kentucky, University of
   College of Architecture
   Lexington, Kentucky 40506-0041

Lawrence Technological University
   College of Architecture and Design
   2100 West Ten Mile Road
   Southfield, Michigan 48075

Louisiana State University
   School of Architecture
   Baton Rouge, Louisiana 70803

Louisiana Tech University
  Department of Architecture
  School of Art and Architecture
  Ruston, Louisiana 71272-3175

Maryland, University of
  School of Architecture
  College Park, Maryland 20742-1411

Massachusetts Institute of Technology
  School of Architecture and Planning
  Department of Architecture
  Cambridge, Massachusetts 02139

Miami University
  Department of Architecture
  School of Fine Arts
  Oxford, Ohio 45056

Miami, University of
  School of Architecture
  Coral Gables, Florida 33146

Michigan, University of
  College of Architecture and Urban Planning
  Ann Arbor, Michigan 48109-2069

Minnesota, University of
  College of Architecture and Landscape Architecture
  Minneapolis, Minnesota 55455

Mississippi State University
  School of Architecture
  Mississippi State, Mississippi 39762

Montana State University
  School of Architecture
  Bozeman, Montana 59717

Nebraska, University of
  College of Architecture
  Lincoln, Nebraska 68588-0106

New Jersey Institute of Technology
  School of Architecture
  Newark, New Jersey 07102

New Mexico, University of
  School of Architecture and Planning
  Albuquerque, New Mexico 87131

New York at Buffalo, State University of
  School of Architecture and Planning
  Buffalo, New York 14214

New York Institute of Technology
  School of Architecture and Fine Arts
  Old Westbury, New York 11568

North Carolina at Charlotte, University of
  College of Architecture
  Charlotte, North Carolina 28223

North Carolina State University
  School of Design, P.O. Box 7701
  Raleigh, North Carolina 27695-7701

North Dakota State University
  Department of Architecture and Landscape Architecture
  Fargo, North Dakota 58105

Notre Dame, University of
  School of Architecture
  Notre Dame, Indiana 46556

Ohio State University
  School of Architecture
  Columbus, Ohio 43210

Oklahoma State University
  School of Architecture
  Stillwater, Oklahoma 74078

Oklahoma, University of
  College of Architecture
  Norman, Oklahoma 73019

Oregon, University of
  Department of Architecture
  Eugene, Oregon 97403

Pennsylvania, University of
  Department of Architecture
  Graduate School of Fine Arts
  Philadelphia, Pennsylvania 19104-6311

Pennsylvania State University
  Department of Architecture
  College of Arts and Architecture
  University Park, Pennsylvania 16802

Pratt Institute
  School of Architecture
  Brooklyn, New York 11205

Princeton University
  School of Architecture
  Princeton, New Jersey 08544-5264

Puerto Rico, University of
  School of Architecture
  Rio Piedras, Puerto Rico 00931

Rensselaer Polytechnic Institute
  School of Architecture
  Troy, New York 12180-3590

Rhode Island School of Design
   Division of Architectural Studies
   Providence, Rhode Island 02903

Rice University
   School of Architecture
   Houston, Texas 77251

Roger Williams College
   Architecture Division
   Bristol, Rhode Island 02809

Southern California, University of
   School of Architecture
   Los Angeles, California 90089-0291

Southern California Institute of Architecture
   1800 Berkeley Street
   Santa Monica, California 90404

Southern University and A & M College
   School of Architecture
   Baton Rouge, Louisiana 70813

Southwestern Louisiana, University of
   School of Art & Architecture
   Lafayette, Louisiana 70504-3850

Syracuse University
   School of Architecture
   Syracuse, New York 13244-1250

Temple University
   Architecture Program
   Department of Engineering
   Philadelphia, Pennsylvania 19122

Tennessee, University of
   School of Architecture
   Knoxville, Tennessee 37996-2400

Texas A & M University
  Department of Architecture
  College Station, Texas 77843-3137

Texas Tech University
  College of Architecture
  Lubbock, Texas 79409-2091

Texas at Arlington, University of
  School of Architecture
  Arlington, Texas 76019

Texas at Austin, University of
  School of Architecture
  Austin, Texas 78712

Tulane University
  School of Architecture
  New Orleans, Louisiana 70118-5671

Tuskegee Institute
  Department of Architecture
  Tuskegee Institute, Alabama 36088

Utah, University of
  Graduate College of Architecture
  Salt Lake City, Utah 84112

Virginia Polytechnic Institute and State University
  College of Architecture and Urban Studies
  Blacksburg, Virginia 24061-0205

Virginia, University of
  School of Architecture
  Charlottesville, Virginia 22903

Washington University
  School of Architecture
  St. Louis, Missouri 63130

Washington, University of
  Department of Architecture
  Seattle, Washington 98195

Washington State University
  School of Architecture
  Pullman, Washington 99164-2220

Wisconsin at Milwaukee, University of
  School of Architecture and Urban Planning
  Milwaukee, Wisconsin 53201

Yale University
  School of Architecture
  New Haven, Connecticut 06511

The 1992 list of Canadian schools is as follows:

University of British Columbia
  School of Architecture
  Vancouver 8, British Columbia V6T 1W5

Carleton University
  School of Architecture
  Ottawa, Ontario K15 5B6

University of Calgary
  Faculty of Environmental Design
  Architecture Program
  Calgary, Canada T2N 1N4

University of Laval
  School of Architecture
  Quebec, Quebec G1K 7P4

University of Manitoba
  Department of Architecture
  Faculty of Architecture
  Winnipeg, Manitoba R3T 2N2

McGill University
  School of Architecture
  Montreal, Quebec H3A 2K6

University of Montreal
  School of Architecture
  Montreal, Quebec H3C 3J7

Nova Scotia Technical, University of
  Faculty of Architecture
  Halifax, Nova Scotia B3J 2X4

University of Toronto
  School of Architecture and Landscape Architecture
  Toronto, Ontario M5S 1A1

In addition to these schools that either have programs accredited by NAAB or that are recognized by the Royal Institute, there are a number of other schools in the United States and Canada that offer some programs in architecture. All are members of the Association of Collegiate Schools of Architecture (ACSA).

ACSA publishes two excellent career documents:

Guide to Architecture Schools in North America will familiarize you with nearly a hundred architectural schools. It provides handy demographic information and statistics.

Life Experiences in Environmental Design will provide information about the work of various people in the profession. It contains a group of fascinating and revealing interviews with young architects who are performing a wide variety of duties in the world of architecture and environmental design.

After reviewing a selection of the materials indicated above, you should then review the catalogs and other materials from schools of interest, consult with your guidance counselor, and secure his or her help in analyzing this information. Your objective should be the selection of those schools most nearly matching your qualifications and interests. Your counselor can be of real assistance in analyzing the details presented in the information you have gathered at this stage.

STUDENT FINANCIAL AID

There are many financial aids and scholarships available to the serious college student. Your guidance counselor will have information on sources and applicant qualifications. An excellent general reference is the publication *Financial Assistance for College Students,* U.S. Government Printing Office, Washington, D.C. 20402. This directory provides information on financial help—loans, scholarships, service grants and aid, and campus employment—which colleges and universities make available to undergraduate and first professional degree students.

A number of other popular financing and scholarship references are available through your local bookstore.

Some such publications cover scholarships exclusively. Further information on this subject is frequently found in appendixes to various college directories published annually and available through retail book outlets.

The American Institute of Architects administers a variety of scholarship programs, available to architecture students on an annual basis. Details of these and other AIA scholarships may be secured by requesting information by writing to the Director of Educational Programs, The American Institute of Architects, 1735 New York Avenue, N.W., Washington, D.C. 20006.

If you are serious about applying for financial assistance or scholarships, it is important to remember that most such awards are given in the spring (usually in April) for the following fall semester. Therefore, applications usually must be filed the previous December through February. In order to gather all the necessary information, it is important that you begin your search for available funding several months prior to these deadlines, or at least a year before the funding will be needed.

INTERNSHIP AND LICENSING REFERENCES

As noted previously, the states and territories have licensing boards that regulate the practice of architecture within their respective jurisdictions. Since architects practice across state lines, all states and territories have reciprocal licensing agreements with other states and territories. The National Council of Architectural Registration Boards (NCARB) promotes uniform licensing procedures and otherwise furthers such reciprocity. There is not, and in all likelihood never will be, a national law regulating the practice of architecture, nor a national license for such practice. However, the NCARB facilitates exchange of an architect's credentials through its programs to develop common licensing procedures.

To round out your view of the licensing requirements governing the practice of architecture, you should secure the name and address of the licensing agency in your state and write for a copy of the rules and regulations pertaining to the examination for and regulation of the practice of architecture. The name and address of the agency may be secured from the office of the city clerk in your home town or the county clerk of your county. Or, you can write directly to the NCARB, 1735 New York Avenue N.W., Washington, D.C. 20006, asking for the name and address of the architectural licensing agency in your state. Licensing regulations of this sort are often written in legal styles and may, at first reading, be difficult to understand. Your guidance counselor can be of assistance in pinpointing those parts of the regulations that will be of greatest interest to you at this point in your search for a career.

PROFESSIONAL REFERENCES

The names and addresses of the principal professional and trade associations that represent the different architectural vocations are listed here. You may wish to write them for additional information on careers in their particular fields.

Architects
> The American Institute of Architects (AIA)
> 1735 New York Avenue N.W.
> Washington, D.C. 20006

Interior Designers
> American Society of Interior Designers (ASID)
> 608 Massachusetts Avenue, N.E.
> Washington, D.C. 20002

Urban Planners
> American Planning Association (APA)
> 1776 Massachusetts Avenue N.W., Suite 704
> Washington, D.C. 20036

Engineering Associations
> American Association of Engineering Societies (AAES)
> 1111 19th Street N.W., Suite 608
> Washington, D.C. 20036

Civil Engineers
> American Society of Civil Engineers (ASCE)
> 345 East 47th Street
> New York, New York 10017

HVAC Engineers
> American Society of Heating, Refrigerating & Air Conditioning Engineers (ASHRAE)

1791 Tullie Circle, N.E.
Atlanta, Georgia 30329

Mechanical Engineers
American Society of Mechanical Engineers (ASME)
345 East 47th Street
New York, New York 10017

Landscape Architects
American Society of Landscape Architects (ASLA)
4401 Connecticut Avenue, N.W.
Washington, D.C. 20008

Consulting Engineers
American Consulting Engineers Council (ACEC)
1015 15th Street N.W.
Washington, D.C. 20005

Electrical Engineers
Institute of Electrical & Electronics Engineers (IEEE)
345 East 47th Street
New York, New York 10017

Lighting Engineers
Illuminating Engineering Society of North America
    (IES)
345 East 47th Street
New York, New York 10017

Engineers
National Society of Professional Engineers
1420 King Street
Alexandria, VA 22314

In writing the design group organizations noted above, you should indicate that you want information on career opportunities in their segment of the construction industry. As you can imagine, some of the organizations represent professionals in other industries as well as construction. For instance, the last organization listed, NSPE, includes in their membership engineers from many different kinds of industries and in both public and private employ.

CONSTRUCTOR GROUP

Careers in general construction contracting
> Associated General Contractors of America, Inc.
> (AGC)
> 1957 E Street N.W.
> Washington, D.C. 20006

Careers in the building trades
> Building & Construction Trades Department
> AFL-CIO
> 815 16th Street N.W.
> Washington, D.C. 20006

Careers in construction specification
> Construction Specifications Institute (CSI)
> 601 Madison Street
> Alexandria, Virginia 22314

Careers in building systems contracting
> Associated Specialty Contractors
> 7315 Wisconsin Avenue
> Bethesda, Maryland 20814

Careers in home building contracting
> National Association of Home Builders (NAHB)
> 15th & M Streets N.W.
> Washington, D.C. 20005

Careers in construction financing
American Bankers Association
1120 Connecticut Avenue N.W.
Washington, D.C. 20036

Careers in construction law
American Bar Association
750 North Lake Shore Drive
Chicago, Illinois 60611

Careers in land and building appraisals
Appraisal Institute
225 North Michigan Avenue, Suite 724
Chicago, Illinois 60601-7601

Careers in insuring construction and building
American Insurance Association
1130 Connecticut Avenue
Washington, D.C. 20036

Careers in building code writing and administration
Building Officials and Code Administrators International (BOCA)
4051 West Flossmoor Road
Country Club Hills, Illinois 60477-5795

International Conference of Building Officials (ICBO)
5360 South Workman Road
Whittier, California 90601

Southern Building Code Congress International (SBCC)
    900 Montclair Road
    Birmingham, Alabama 35213

Careers in building research
    Building Research Board
    2101 Constitution Avenue N.W.
    Washington, D.C. 20062

Careers in all elements of the construction industry
    Chamber of Commerce of the United States
      Community Resources Development Center
    1615 H Street N.W.
    Washington, D.C. 20062

Careers in real estate
    National Association of Realtors
    430 North Michigan Avenue
    Chicago, Illinois 60611

Careers in facility management
    International Facility Management Association
      (IFMA)
    1 East Greenway Plaza, 11th Floor
    Houston, Texas 77046

Federal government careers in design & construction
    Office of Personnel Management
    1900 E Street N.W.
    Washington, D.C. 20415-0001

Careers in community development
    Urban Land Institute (ULD)
    625 Indiana Avenue, N.W.
    Washington, D.C. 20004

Careers in construction financing
United States League of Savings Institutions
1709 New York Avenue, N.W., Suite 801
Washington, D.C. 20006

In writing any of the above support group organizations, you should indicate to them that you want information on career opportunities in that segment of the construction industry they represent. As you can imagine, some of these organizations have many interests outside the construction industry. The U.S. Civil Service Commission, for example, represents federal employees in all government agencies.

In your pursuit of career choices no doubt you have uncovered many, many possibilities and want further information. Your school's guidance counselor is, of course, your first resource. Other excellent resources are the national professional associations devoted to advancing the art, the science, and the business practices of each particular segment of our nation's culture and economy. There are thousands of such associations and each is eager to introduce the young person to career opportunities within the segment of national life they represent. These associations are listed, along with their addresses, telephone numbers and a brief explanation of their various purposes in one generally available reference: *The Encyclopedia of Associations,* 26th Edition, 1992, Gale Research Company, Detroit, Michigan. This reference should be available in most public libraries.

VGM CAREER HORIZONS PUBLICATIONS

Finally, you should note that VGM Career Horizons, the publisher of this manual on career opportunities in architecture, publishes a number of similar career guidance manuals relating to other environmental design professions such as those discussed throughout this book. Information on these publications can be secured by writing VGM Career Horizons, NTC Publishing Group, 4255 W. Touhy Avenue, Lincolnwood, Illinois 60646.

BIBLIOGRAPHY OF RELATED READINGS

An American Architecture, Frank Lloyd Wright, 1955.

Appraisal of Real Estate, 7th ed., American Institute of Real Estate Appraisers, editors, (Ballinger: 1978)

Architect? A Candid Guide to the Profession. MIT Press. (Cambridge, Massachusetts: 1988).

An Architect—The First Ten Years, John Donaghey, John Donaghey Publications. (Garland, Texas: 1980).

Architect's Technical Reference, E.D. Mills, Robert E. Krieger Publishing Co. (Huntington, NY: 1976)

Architecture, The World Book Encyclopedia, Volume 1, World Book, Incorporated, (Chicago: 1992).

Architecture—A Place for Women, Ellen Perry Berkely, ed., Smithsonian Institution Press (Washington: 1989).

Architecture as Space, Bruno Zevi, Horizons (New York: 1975)

Architectural and Building Trades Dictionary, 3rd ed., Robert Putnam and G.E. Carlson, Van Nostrand Reinhold (New York: 1983)

Architectural Drafting, J.H. Earle. Creative Publishing Company (College Station, Texas: 1975)

Architectural Drafting and Design, 6th ed., Ernest Weidhaas, Prentice Hall (New York: 1989)

Architectural Drawing, 3rd. ed., Lawton M. Patten and Roth G. Kendall, Hunt Publishing Co. (Dubuque, Iowa: 1991)

Architectural Photography, 3rd ed., John Veltri, American Photographic Book Publishing Co. (Garden City, NY: 1975)

Basic Blueprint Reading & Sketching, 5th ed., C. Thomas Olivio et. al., Delmar (Albany, NY: 1988)

The Book of Landscape Design, Ortloff and Raymore, M. Barrow (New York: 1959)

Building: The Fight Against Gravity, Mario Salvadori, Atheneum (New York: 1979)

Design and Detail of the Space Between Buildings, Elizabeth Beazley, Architectural Press (London: 1960)

Design: Purpose, Form and Meaning, University of Massachusetts Press (Amherst, Massachusetts: 1979)

Dwelling House Construction, 5th ed., Albert G.H. Dietz, MIT Press, (Cambridge, Massachusetts: 1990)

Experiencing Architecture, Steen Eiler Rasmussen, MIT Press (Cambridge: 1980)

Freehand Sketching, 2nd ed., Joseph W. Giachino and Henry J. Beukema, American Technical Publishers (Homewood, Illinois: 1978)

House, Tracy Kidder, Houghton Mifflin Company (Boston: 1985)

Houses—The Illustrated Guide to Construction, Design and Systems, 2nd ed. Henry S. Harrison, Dearborn Financial Publishing Incorporated (Chicago: 1991)

How Architecture Works, Douglas E. Gordon and Stephanie Stubbs, Van Nostrand Reinhold (New York: 1991)

How Buildings Work, Edward Allen, Oxford University Press, (New York: 1980)

Interior Design: An Introduction to Architectural Interiors, 3rd
   ed., Arnold Friedmann, John Pile and Wilson Forest,
   Elsevier Science, 1982.
An Introduction to Landscape Architecture, Michael Laurie,
   Elsevier Science (New York: 1985)
An Introduction to the Study of Landscape Design, Hubbard
   and Kimball, originally published by Macmillan (New York:
   1917) and republished by Hubbard Educational Trust, Inc.
   (Boston: 1959)
Kindergarten Chats and Other Writings, Louis Sullivan, Dover
   (New York: 1979)
*Landscape and Human Life, the Impact of Landscape
   Architecture Upon Human Activities,* International Federation
   of Landscape Architects (Amsterdam: 1966)
Neighborhood Space, Randolph Hester, Dowden, Hutchison &
   Ross, Inc. (Stroudsburg, Pennsylvania)
Opportunities in Landscape Architecture, Ralph Griswold and
   William Swain, NTC Publishing Group (Lincolnwood,
   Illinois: 1987)
Shaping Tomorrow's Landscape, Sylvia Crowe and Zvi Miller,
   Djambatan, (Amsterdam: 1964)
Space for Living, Sylvia Crowe, Djambatan, (Amsterdam: 1961)
Space, Time and Architecture, 5th ed., Sigfried Giedien,
   Harvard University Press, (Cambridge, Massachusetts: 1967)